D1591664

ELEMENTARY 1
PERSPECTIVES

Teaching Concepts
of
Peace and Conflict

William J. Kreidler

Educators for Social Responsibility
23 Garden Street
Cambridge, MA 02138

Published 1990. Second Edition 1991.
Printed in the United States of America
95 94 93   5

ISBN 0-942349-01-6

Designed by Jane Cook

Illustrations by Rosemary Ladd-Griffin

CONTENTS

FOREWORD

Writing the foreword to this book gives me the opportunity to pay tribute to a dedicated group of educators who launched ESR in the early eighties.

Educators for Social Responsibility's purpose is to make social responsibility an integral part of education. Social responsibility is seen to be an integrating framework for a variety of activities that will help young people learn how to participate in shaping a better world.

ESR was born out of concern about the danger of nuclear war. The nuclear arms race was a highly controversial subject, usually avoided by schools in spite of the accumulating evidence that it was having a significant impact on the lives of children. During the summer of 1982 the Boston Area Chapter of ESR, under the inspired leadership of Shelley Berman, created a curriculum—*Dialogue: A Teaching Guide to Nuclear Issues*—to provide educators with some guidelines and strategies for listening to student concerns and teaching about this sensitive topic.

Next the Boston group tackled a new question: "How do we build the bridge between preventing nuclear war and creating and preserving peace?" Shelley Berman initiated a series of interviews with students, teachers, and administrators. Four striking conclusions resulted.

- While students had a concrete concept of war, their concept of peace was often abstract, or simply the absence of war.
- Students had a clear image of the Soviets as "the enemy" and held deep prejudices based on little information.
- Students expressed a strong sense of powerlessness and lack of inspiring models of individuals and organizations that had made a difference.
- Adolescents, who are naturally idealistic, were instead expressing a cynicism about the possibilities for a better future.

Here was another challenge—to produce a curriculum addressing these needs. Again, as in the previous summer with *Dialogue*, a group of teachers worked to produce a new curriculum: *Perspectives: A Teaching Guide to Concepts of Peace*. Over seventy teachers and parents participated in its writing. The project brought people together to think through hard issues and together they produced a powerful and influential book of curriculum ideas. Furthermore, it was an experience that gave the participants a special sense of enrichment and empowerment.

A group effort needs leadership to encourage participation and editorship to create a coherent result. Shelley provided both, but a special tribute is also due to Susan Jones. She did outstanding work editing the elementary section and assisting throughout the book.

The original *Perspectives* was important as a teaching guide, but also significant is the fact that, together with *Dialogue* it gave substance to a fledgling organization and enabled it to survive and grow. It is an important part of ESR's history.

Perspectives: A Teaching Guide to Concepts of Peace is a forerunner to this present book. Not long after the publication of *Perspectives*, ESR began to discuss plans for revising it. An initial revision group consisting of Susan Jones, Shelley Berman, William J. Kreidler, and Cheryl Klausner was formed. They carefully considered the feedback from teachers and leading peace educators and discussed how a revised *Perspectives* might look. This group laid a foundation for the current revision.

The world has entered a new era in international relations since *Perspectives* and *Dialogue* were developed. Peace remains a vital concept, both internationally and (perhaps most urgent these days) domestically. Elementary teachers continue to ask ESR for materials that will help them work with their students to understand and think constructively about peace, war, violence, conflict, justice, enemies, and other complex and very current concerns.

Given this clear need, ESR asked William J. Kreidler to pick up and complete the task of rewriting *Perspectives*, tailoring it to the particular needs of elementary teachers and students. Drawing on his considerable experience as a classroom teacher and curriculum developer, Bill has created a teaching guide that retains the spirit and heart of the original *Perspectives*, but carries it into the 1990s.

In addition to this overview about the history of the book, I wish to add a personal observation. I was involved on the periphery of the original *Perspectives* effort, but close enough to experience the surge of excitement and commitment that Shelley created and the response in achievement that he inspired from a dedicated group of colleagues. I was impressed then, and I am impressed now, by the searching mind and driving energy Shelley brings to bear on ESR work.

Richmond Mayo-Smith
Chairman of the Board
Educators for Social Responsibility

ACKNOWLEDGMENTS

A book like this does not happen without the contributions and support of many people. I would like to thank some of them here. First, I want to thank the team of teachers and writers who developed the first edition of *Perspectives*. They are the ones who created the material from which I worked. In particular I would like to thank those who have worked most closely with me over the years: Shelley Berman, Susan Jones, Cheryl Klausner, and Fern Fisher worked with me during the early stages of this revision. Shelley Berman, in addition to editing the original *Perspectives*, convened the group that first thought about how this revision might look. His energy and support over the years have been invaluable, and I thank him. Susan Jones' insights and ideas are evident throughout *Elementary Perspectives 1*. The following activities were adapted from materials developed by Susan Jones: Pieces of Peace, Peace and the Environment, It Isn't Fair!, If I Were in Charge, Peace Symbols, Squiggle Drawing, Villains are Human Too, and Appendix A: Teaching Controversial Issues to Elementary Children. Susan also created the illustrations on pages 35 and 36. I greatly appreciate her contributions and her friendship. Sarah Pirtle developed many of the activities in chapter 1 and elsewhere and was instrumental in helping me conceptualize this revision.

I owe an enormous debt to my reviewers: Sonia Ebel, Oakland, California Public Schools; Ellen Davidson, teacher, educator, and author; Sara Goodman, Boston Area Educators for Social Responsibility; Sarah Pirtle, teacher, writer, and songwriter; Carol Reid, Charlotte, North Carolina Public Schools; Jay Scoggins, Minneapolis, Minnesota Public Schools.

Each of them is thoroughly grounded in classroom practice and each went through the manuscript page by page, testing activities, suggesting both revisions and new possibilities. Their practical and philosophical feedback, combined with their enthusiasm and care for the project, was immensely helpful and inspirational.

I also want to thank the following people for their support and enthusiasm, both for the project and for me personally: Nancy and Ted Graves, with their expertise in cooperative learning; Barbara Bond and Melania Bruno for their experience in multicultural education and prejudice reduction; Petra Hesse for her insights on children and enemies; and

Nancy Schniedewind for her thoughtful contributions on cooperation and community as values. Thanks also to David Hyerle, Nancy Carlsson-Paige, Diane Levin, Gail Sadalla, Ann Gibson, Priscilla Prutzman, Rich Cohen, Steve Weimar, Dell Salza, and Larry Dieringer for support, good ideas, and hard questions when needed.

I'd especially like to thank my co-worker Rachel Poliner, who took over some of my duties while I finished the book. I'd like to thank all my friends, particularly David Aronstein, for putting up with it.

Thank you to the students I work with at the Agassiz Elementary School in Jamaica Plain, Massachusetts, and at the Driscoll School in Brookline, Massachusetts. You were the guinea pigs. And finally, my thanks to the many teachers with whom I've worked. Your questions, ideas, and dedication to your work keep me inspired.

INTRODUCTION

I spend a lot of time in schools, and I often hear--or overhear--some pretty remarkable things. I'll always remember walking down a hallway in one elementary school and hearing the shouts of a teacher who had obviously reached the end of her rope: "If I don't get some peace in this room, you kids won't have recess for the rest of your LIVES!" There followed the kind of quiet that is known as pin-drop quiet. Even I, out in the hall, didn't dare make a sound. But was there peace in that room for either the children or the teacher?

What is peace? We hear the word used in a variety of ways, in a variety of contexts, by a variety of people. To one person peace is a long afternoon on a deserted beach, to another it's a night on the town in the company of good friends, to a third it's living in a nation thriving in the absence of war, to a fourth it's a sense of personal safety and security. "Peace" means something different to each of us. It's a collection of concepts, and our personal definitions are made up of our attitudes, experiences, feelings, behaviors, and moods.

If peace is so complex an idea, can it be taught? Exactly what do we teach when we teach about peace? *Elementary Perspectives 1* is a resource guide for elementary teachers or anyone who works with children in grades K to 6. It is based on several beliefs. The first is that children and adults should be encouraged to explore the concepts of peace and to develop their personal definitions of peace. Second, the attitudes, thoughts, feelings, and behaviors that make up those definitions should be examined. Third, there are skills that are commonly agreed upon as being a part of the definition of peace, and those skills can be taught. Finally, by examining obstacles to peace and the opposite of peace, we learn something about what peace means.

HOW TO USE THIS BOOK

This book is designed to be used easily by you in your work with children. It is a resource guide of activities related to the concept of peace. The activities are not, for the most part, sequenced, and they can be used singly to introduce concepts or ideas, or to supplement other lessons. Activities can also be grouped into a unit of study on peace and related concepts. Many teachers are setting aside time weekly or even daily to practice such peace-related skills as cooperation and conflict resolution. This book offers activities for these sessions.

Each activity contains:

• Grade levels from K to 6. Grade levels in parentheses signal that the activity can be adapted to either higher or lower grade levels.
• Objectives that describe the goals of the activity.
• Subject areas into which the activity can fit.
• Materials needed, including the enclosed worksheets or handouts, which follow the activity.
• Instructions on how to conduct the activity.
• Discussion questions to help deepen student learning.
• "Going Further" suggestions for ways to build on the activity.
• Worksheets and/or handouts for the activity, when required.

Some of the activities are designed using a cooperative learning model, and to use these effectively your students will need to be familiar with this approach. If you want to know more about how to implement cooperative learning, check the list of resources in Appendix B. Most of the activities can be done cooperatively or not, depending upon your assessment of what would be the most effective use of the activity at any particular time. Activities that require advance preparation, more than one session, or prerequisites are identified in the instructions.

I have chosen several broad categories as a framework for organizing the concepts of peace. They are not strictly defined, but overlap, interact, and work together to give students the broadest possible concept of peace.

Each chapter contains a basic concept and poses, directly or indirectly, several questions related to that concept.

Chapter 1 What is Peace?

What does "peace" mean? What are its dynamic qualities? How does the concept of justice change or enhance the meaning of peace? What is non-peace or the lack of peace?

Chapter 2 Peace and Community Building

What qualities are present in a community? How do people solve the problems that arise working in groups? What does community mean at different levels?

Chapter 3 Peace and Conflict

What causes conflict and what makes it get worse? How can conflict be used productively? Can conflict and peace enhance each other? Why understand various perspectives in conflict? What is societal conflict?

Chapter 4 Peace and Diversity

How are we diverse? How does diversity enrich us? How does it cause problems? What are stereotypes, prejudices, discrimination? How do we acquire prejudices and how do they hurt us? How are they obstacles to peace?

Chapter 5 Peace and Enemies

What are enemies? How are our perceptions of enemies related to prejudices, stereotypes, and propaganda? What are nonviolent ways people have stood up to evil actions in the world?

Chapter 6 Visions of Peace

What would a peaceful world look like? How have artists and others envisioned peace throughout the years? How do I envision a world at peace?

WHY TEACH CONCEPTS OF PEACE?

People sometimes ask, "Why teach about peace? Kids just know what peace is." Several years ago, the Boston chapter of Educators for Social Responsibility conducted a study by interviewing students, teachers, and administrators on the subject of peace. The results were startling. While students had concrete concepts of war as some-thing exciting and glamorous, their conception of peace was often abstract, vaguely defined as simply the absence of war. Peace was often perceived of as weak, passive, dull, and boring. In addition, while students usually had clear ideas about enemies, they were based on deep and unquestioned prejudices, not on information. Finally, students had little under-standing of the peacemaking process and a strong sense of powerlessness concerning the future. They expressed little hope for lasting peace.

It was in an effort to address these concerns that the original edition of *Perspectives* was developed in 1984. It was the direct result of ESR's efforts to find balanced and devel-opmentally appropriate activities for teaching about nuclear war and its prevention--a topic that was much discussed at the time, both within and outside schools. Since then there have been several encouraging developments, including the slowing of the nuclear arms race and improvements in international relations.

But there is still a clear need for students to learn about peace. Looking at our classrooms, our schools, our communities, our nation, and the world, there is abundant evidence that violence is escalating and that peace continues to elude us. Young people still express feelings of hopelessness about the possibility of peace at any level--personal, interpersonal, or international. Peace still needs to be put forth as something valued, worth learning about, worth working for.

THE WORKING DEFINITION

Having just said that peace means something different to everyone, I want to tell you the definition I used in developing the material in this book.

Peace is that state when all people are able to survive and thrive without being hampered by conflict, prejudice, enmity, or injustice. Peace is most likely to exist in the context of a community that includes caring, cooperation, communication, appreciation for diversity, and appropriate emotional expression. Peace is a realistic and attainable goal. It is also an inspiring ideal.

I don't think you can teach anything without your values showing, and certainly not a concept as complex and personal as peace. I want to be clear about the values and be-liefs behind *Elementary Perspectives 1*. The book is rooted in the traditional values of caring, compassion, community, fairness, and responsibility for individual actions. It grows from the belief that:

- Peace is always a worthy goal
- Peace is dynamic, not static
- Conflict can have positive results
- Conflict can be resolved to the benefit of all
- Community is the context most conducive to dynamic peace
- The world is a community and all its people are interconnected
- Real peace is dependent on justice
- Nonviolence is preferable to violence
- Current social conflicts should be discussed in classrooms in ways that are balanced and developmentally appropriate
- Children need to learn to participate responsibly in democracy
- Children need models of how people have confronted evil in the world

THE PEDAGOGY OF *ELEMENTARY PERSPECTIVES 1*

The activities in *Elementary Perspectives 1: Teaching Concepts of Peace and Conflict* are designed to help students define peace according to their own values, to examine their definitions from many angles, and to learn the concrete skills involved in living according to those definitions. The activities reflect the pedagogy of Educators for Social Responsibility. It is a pedagogy based on cooperative problem solving, conflict resolution, listening to other points of view, community building, decision making, and critical thinking. In *Elementary Perspectives 1* this means that the starting point is always listening to the children's own experiences and helping them to reflect on and generalize from that experience. The next step is to help them to expand their concepts beyond their own experience. Then we help children to make connections at levels other than the personal: local, national, and international. Finally, we empower children by encouraging them to take appropriate responsible actions based on their beliefs. Not all activities accomplish all of these objectives, of course, but all of the activities fit within this pedagogical framework.

You, as the teacher, play the key role in implementing this pedagogy. For the activities in *Elementary Perspectives 1* to be most effective, it is helpful for you to keep in mind the following principles of good teaching.

Listen to the children. Listening is one of the cornerstones of *Elementary Perspectives 1*, especially listening to children's experiences and feelings and then helping them to reflect on and learn from those experiences. Helping children learn to listen carefully and with empathy to each other is another common theme in the activities.

The classroom is a caring community. Community provides a context that makes concepts of peace meaningful and real. Children don't learn such concepts as listening, caring, cooperative problem solving, and conflict resolution by hearing about them, but by experiencing them. Indeed, the classroom and the school may be the only place in which some students encounter concepts of peace. As teachers, we set the tone for caring and community in the classroom.

The children are watching us. Modeling the behavior we want is one of the ways we encourage that behavior in children. If we want caring listening, peaceful conflict resolution, community building, and appreciation for diversity, we must model those. That doesn't mean that every time we have a conflict with a child we have to negotiate a solution; that is neither possible nor appropriate. But we do need to be aware of our own behavior, which should be generally consistent with what we ask the children to do.

Teach discussion skills. Hearing other people's ideas helps children shape and sharpen their own. Much of this sharing of ideas happens in discussions. It will take time and effort on your part, but in my experience children can learn the skills required for good discussions. I've found that a simple set of rules helps:

• One person talks at a time. Let people finish what they say. (If necessary, use a prop, such as holding a feather or ball to indicate whose turn it is to speak.)
• Respect what others say. Don't laugh at or ridicule what they say. If you disagree with someone, say so without putting them down.
• Say what has happened to you or what you think. Talk from your own perspective.

Help students learn to live with ambiguity. Children sometimes have difficulty with activities in which there is not one clear, correct answer. They may need reassurance with the activities in *Elementary Perspectives 1* that there can be many "right" answers. For your part, accept a variety of answers. What is important are the thinking skills students demonstrate. When students don't have much experience with open-ended questions or activities, they will sometimes try to pass off slipshod work or ideas not well thought out. You may need to watch for and correct this tendency.

SOME PRACTICAL CONSIDERATIONS

Will it be controversial?

This book is based on the idea that peace is desirable. It is *how* to achieve peace that is controversial. It would be naive to pretend that the topic of peace is not going to be controversial.

My own experience teaching in a variety of communities has been that parents don't, as a rule, object to teachers bringing up the topic of peace or related concepts. They do object to their children being propagandized or frightened. And they object to their own teaching being undermined or devalued. To create a climate of trust for your activities:

• Use your experience in the community to assess community standards. You may also want to talk to other teachers and administrators. There may be some activities that it would be better to omit or adapt.
• Let parents know what you are doing. A brief explanation of the activities in a newsletter to parents can prevent misunderstandings and hard feelings. Explain how the activities fit into the curriculum.
• Involve parents in the activities when you can. Encourage children to solicit their parents' opinions.
• If parents do have objections to an activity, listen to and be respectful of their concerns. You may need to offer to let their child sit out a particular activity.

For approaches to using controversy in the elementary curriculum, see Appendix A.

Where Do I Find Time to Teach This?

We have busy days in our classrooms, and finding time to squeeze in one more thing seems just about impossible. The activities in *Elementary Perspectives 1* are designed to fit into your standard curriculum. I have found it useful to create units tied to social studies, reading, or health, so I could bring the material into the curriculum in a natural way. For example, activities on stereotyping and prejudice are a good springboard for a unit on the civil rights movement in American history. Many of the activities can be used by themselves and added to a particular unit of study. There are many writing activities that can be used as in-class or homework assignments. For example, if the class is working on paragraphing, students can write a paragraph about their vision of a peaceful world and what it would look like.

The activities in *Elementary Perspectives 1* are strongest in the social studies/language arts/arts areas; forthcoming curricular materials from Educators for Social Responsibility will focus on mathematics and science. Appendix B lists trade books that deal with peace or peace-related themes. These books can be very useful for bringing concepts of peace into the curriculum.

GOING FURTHER

The focus of this book, as the subtitle suggests, is teaching concepts of peace and conflict. That covers a lot of ground, and to keep the book from becoming too broad and too inclusive, I had to resist the temptation to explore the many fascinating topics and issues that are related to studying peace.

As a teacher, you don't have that problem. Many of the topics raised in this book-- such as conflict resolution, cooperative learning, prejudice and stereotyping, global educa- tion--can be examined in multiple contexts and invite exploration in greater depth than the activities in this book allow. (Appendix C lists curricula and teacher resources that will be helpful.) Similarly, as you and your students do the activities in *Elementary Perspectives 1*, related topics may very well come up, particularly social issues like hunger, homelessness, and discrimination. I sincerely hope that the topic of peace will serve as a springboard for you and your students.

We are interested in hearing how *Elementary Perspectives 1* works for you. There is a feedback form at the end of this book. Good luck!

Chapter One:
WHAT IS PEACE?

INTRODUCTION

According to the *MacMillan Beginning Dictionary*, "peace" is "freedom from fighting" or "a lack of noise or disorder." Peace is usually defined this way, as the absence of something, such as war, conflict, fighting, or chaos; or it is defined as quiet, serenity, calmness. There is nothing wrong with these definitions, as far as they go, but they make peace sound boring, as if it were a vacuum created by the absence of something stimulating.

If peace is freedom from fighting, for example, just what is going on instead of fighting? Square-dancing? Videogames? Quilting? The activities in this chapter encourage children to define peace by what it is, rather than by what it is not. They are based on the assumption that when people are not fighting they are free to do a host of interesting and exciting things-- far more than sitting around being quiet and serene.

The first set of activities (numbers 1-8) focuses on developing personal definitions of peace by exploring personal experiences with peace. The second set (numbers 9-15) encourages more complex definitions by challenging students to think about the opposite of peace and to include social justice and environmental awareness in their concept of peace. The third set of activities (numbers 16-18) encourages students to expand their definitions by considering how other cultures and languages symbolize peace.

Teaching Considerations

Throughout the activities in this and other chapters, try to emphasize peace as a bold, dynamic, and exciting concept.
• In this chapter, students will be developing personal definitions of peace that will vary in scope. Be accepting of them. For example, for one student peace maintained by nuclear threat will still be peace, whereas for another student it will not be. What is important is the thinking that goes into developing the definitions, not so much the definitions themselves.

- If this is your students' first experience in defining a concept as complex and broad as peace, they may become frustrated with the ambiguities of the process and confused about how different people could have different definitions of the same word. Point out the similarities in all the definitions in addition to acknowledging the differences. Don't do all the activities in this chapter at once. Spread them out and try interspersing activities from other chapters that deal with other aspects of peace and non-peace.
- Examining the opposite of peace–war, violence, conflict, etc.–is an important part of helping students refine their definitions of peace. So is exploring various obstacles to peace.

Connecting to Larger Issues

Encourage students to apply their definitions of peace to local, national, and world peace. Asking such questions as "Can you think of an example between countries?" or "Have you seen that happen in our town?" can help students begin to make these connections.

- You can also help students make connections to larger issues by supplying examples yourself. Bring in current-event stories or pictures from magazines that illustrate ideas the children raise. Encourage them to do the same.

PICTURING PEACE:
What Peace Feels Like to Me

GRADE LEVELS: K-6

OBJECTIVES: To develop definitions of "peace" that are based on personal experience

SUBJECT AREAS: Language arts, social studies

MATERIALS: Drawing paper, crayons

INSTRUCTIONS

1. Ask students: Remember a time you felt peace. What were you doing? Were you playing a game? Making Something? Were you alone? With your family? Your friends? Were you inside or outside? Think of the time as if it were a photograph. Remember the setting, the colors, the smells, the way your body was positioned. Try to put yourself back into that time.

2. Have students draw a picture of the scene they remember, including all the vivid details. Some pictures will be highly detailed, others very impressionistic. (If students remembered several incidents, they may draw more than one picture.)

3. Have students share their drawings and describe the times they have felt peace. (Leave open the option of passing, as some students may draw scenes they decide are too personal to share with the class.)

DISCUSSION QUESTIONS

- Are there things that all the pictures have in common? What themes did you see repeated often?
- How were the memories/pictures different from each other?
- How do you think the other people represented in your picture were feeling? Would they say the experience was peace?
- Is there a difference between feeling peace and feeling at peace or feeling peaceful? If so, what is it?
- Can you think of other times when peace felt different from the time you described?

2 PEACE STORM: Brainstorming Peace

GRADE LEVELS: 2-6

OBJECTIVES: To explore associations and concepts of peace; to identify what is opposite of peace

SUBJECT AREAS: Language arts, social studies

MATERIALS: Chalkboard and chalk or large sheets of paper and markers

INSTRUCTIONS

1. Provide space for recording two long lists. First have the class brainstorm the words they have heard in connection with peace. This means writing a list of the contributions without evaluation. Next, in a separate area record all the images and words that come to mind which relate to war or violence.

2. Give the group a chance to stand back and think critically about the words assembled on both sides. Clarify vocabulary that may not be familiar such as "tranquil" or "pacifist."

3. An alternate way to record the responses is by using a web chart, in which words the children associate with peace are written around the central word and connected visually to it or to each other as they come up (see the illustration below). This method of recording word associations is more dynamic than a simple list, as it can show the connections among the various concepts that arise in the course of the brainstorming.

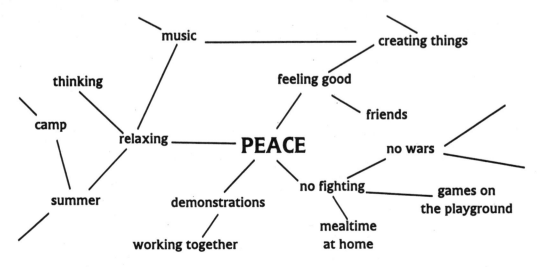

DISCUSSION QUESTIONS

- Are the words representing excitement and activity mostly under the heading of "violence?"
- Do most of the peace words relate to quiet, harmony, stillness?
- Does peace mean "peace and quiet," or can peace be active and exciting?
- Has anyone ever told you that peace will never work? What do you think this means?
- We said the opposite of peace was war (or violence). What are some other words that describe the opposite of peace?

3 PEACE STORM PLUS

GRADE LEVELS: K-6

OBJECTIVES: To expand the definition of "peace" to include exciting and challenging activities

SUBJECT AREAS: Language arts

MATERIALS: Chalkboard and chalk or newsprint/large sheets of paper and markers

INSTRUCTIONS

1. Ask students to brainstorm exciting, thrilling, fun things to do. List these on the chalkboard or on newsprint. Examples might be climbing a mountain, a snowball fight, flying an airplane, riding a roller coaster, going to a birthday party. Stop the brainstorm after ten or fifteen items.

2. Discuss each item on the list using the questions below. Help students identify the conditions that would be necessary for a particular activity to be "peaceful."

DISCUSSION QUESTIONS

- What things about this activity are peaceful?
- What things about this activity are not peaceful?
- How could this activity be done in a way that is (even more) peaceful?

4 PEACEFUL VERBS

GRADE LEVELS: 2-5

OBJECTIVES: To reinforce the concept of dynamic peace

SUBJECT AREAS: Language arts

MATERIALS: Handout 1-4: "Peaceful Verbs"; optional: *The Happy Owls* by Celestino Patti

INSTRUCTIONS

1. Review the definition of a verb: an action word.

2. Have students work in groups of four. Give each group handout 2-4: "Peaceful Verbs." Ask each group to fill in each space with a "peaceful verb," that is, an action word that denotes something that is peaceful. Groups may list more than one word per letter. Upon completion, each group member should sign the handout.

3. Have a spokesperson from each group share his or her group's handout. One way to do this is to have each group pantomime the verbs recorded for a letter of the alphabet. The rest of the class can guess the verb. Discuss the handout. You might want to take this opportunity to discuss the cooperative process: problems that arose, how decisions were made, etc.

4. With younger children you can read *The Happy Owls* by Celestino Patti, in which the owls explain to the barnyard animals why they never fight: there are too many other things they like to do. This book is an excellent introduction to Handout 1-4: "Peaceful Verbs."

DISCUSSION QUESTIONS

- For which letters on the handout was it most easy to think of words? For which was it most difficult?
- As a group, how did you choose words for the easy letters?
- How did you find verbs for the difficult letters?
- What was something you did well as a group?
- What was something you could do better another time?

GOING FURTHER

There are a number of traditional word games that can be adapted to this topic. One is to have students write the word P E A C E down the side of a sheet of paper. Next to each letter, have them list peaceful verbs that begin with P, E, A, etc. Or, instead of peaceful verbs, have them write words that are related to peace that begin with the appropriate letter.

Another variation is to make a class "Peaceful Verbs Book." Have students work in small groups, and assign each group two or three letters. For each letter give them an 11 x 16 piece of construction paper, along with magazines, scissors, and paste. For each letter the group should make a collage of peaceful activities that begin with that letter. Group members should sign the pages they create. When all the groups have finished, all the pages can be bound together into a book.

Handout 1-4
PEACEFUL VERBS

Verbs are action words. They are words that tell things people can do. With some friends, think of a verb for each letter of the alphabet. Make them peaceful verbs, things you would rather do than fight.

A _____   N _____

B _____   O _____

C _____   P _____

D _____   Q _____

E _____   R _____

F _____   S _____

G _____   T _____

H _____   U _____

I _____   V _____

J _____   W _____

K _____   X _____

L _____   Y _____

M _____   Z _____

5 DRAWING DYNAMIC PEACE

GRADE LEVELS: K-6

OBJECTIVES: To reinforce the concept of dynamic peace through cooperative drawing; to build community through a cooperatively structured activity

SUBJECT AREAS: Language arts; social studies

MATERIALS: Large sheets of paper for each group and crayons or markers

INSTRUCTIONS

This activity is cooperatively structured. You may want to provide your class with practice in cooperative group decision making before you attempt this. As an example, see Activity 2-11: "Practicing Group Decision Making" in chapter 2.

1. Divide students into groups of four. Supply each group with large paper and drawing supplies. Explain to them that they will be creating one large scene showing as many people as they can fit on the paper engaging in peaceful activities.

2. Have the group members discuss the things they want to show and who wants to draw them. Ask them to determine the things they want to have in the background–the natural objects or buildings or other human-made things that would need to be in the picture. They should first decide on the placement of mountains, lakes, houses, etc. before drawing the figures so everyone in the group has one congruent landscape to work on.

3. When they are finished, ask them to put a title on their drawing and have everyone in the group sign his or her name.

DISCUSSION QUESTIONS

- What did you include in your drawing?
- In what ways are the activities represented peaceful?
- How did your group decide what to include in your drawing?
- What problems arose as you worked together? How did you solve them?
- What would you like someone to learn from looking at your drawing?
- What do you learn from looking at this group's drawing?
- What is something you did well as a group?
- What could you do better next time?

6 PEACE COMPARISONS

GRADE LEVELS: K-6

OBJECTIVES: To explore the concept of peace by developing analogies and metaphors

SUBJECT AREAS: Thinking skills, language arts

MATERIALS: Handout 1-6: "Peace Comparisons" or alternative described below

INSTRUCTIONS

1. Explain that it is fun to compare things to each other and that doing so "stretches" the imagination.

2. Offer some warm-up questions to introduce and reinforce the idea that there is no one correct answer and to get your students' imaginations working: What color is happiness? What kind of animal is cooperation? What form of water is anger?

3. After the class has done several comparisons together, have older students complete Handout 1-6: "Peace Comparisons." This can be done in cooperative groups, pairs, or individually. When they have finished, have them share their responses with the class.

4. For younger students, label large sheets of paper with the questions from the handout. Read the questions and record the class contributions under the appropriate heading.

Handout 1-6
PEACE COMPARISONS

What animal is peace? _____

What size is peace? _____

What does peace taste like? _____

What form of transportation is peace?_____

If water were peace, what would it be doing?_____

Red is like peace because _____

Brown is like peace because_____

Green is like peace because _____

A waterfall is like peace because _____

A rainstorm is like peace because _____

A river is like peace because _____

A kite flying is like peace because _____

Beavers are like peace because_____

A lion is like peace because _____

A wolf is like peace because _____

Bananas are like peace because _____

Peace is like _____ because _____

_____

7 HELPING HANDS FOR PEACE

GRADE LEVELS: K-3

OBJECTIVES: To identify peaceful and nonpeaceful activities; to link helping others with the concept of peace

SUBJECT AREAS: Language arts, art

MATERIALS: Construction paper, scissors, crayons

INSTRUCTIONS

1. Begin by discussing the concept of helping. Ask: what are some ways you help other people in school? At home? In the community?

2. Give each child a piece of construction paper. Have the children trace both of their hands and then cut out the outline. On each cutout have children write their names. On each finger have them write a way in which they help other people.

3. Very young children may write just one helping activity on each cutout.

4. Mount the cutouts on a "Helping Hands for Peace" bulletin board. Follow up the activity by playing a helping game such as Activity 2-6: "Frozen Beanbag."

5. Have students identify peaceful and nonpeaceful activities and write them on the fingers of the cutouts.

DISCUSSION QUESTIONS

· What does helping other people have to do with peace?
· What are some times other people have helped you?
· What would you say to someone you wanted to help?
· What would you say if you were asking for help?

GOING FURTHER

Read students the poem "Helping" on page 101 of *Where the Sidewalk Ends* by Shel Silverstein.

8 PEACE INTERVIEW

GRADE LEVELS: 2-6

OBJECTIVES: To interview older people about peace; to expand personal definitions of peace by hearing those of other people

SUBJECT AREAS: Language arts, social studies

MATERIALS: Handout 1-8: "Peace Interviews" (or you may prefer to have the class devise one of its own)

INSTRUCTIONS

1. Begin by dividing students into pairs and having them interview each other using Handout 1-8: "Peace Interviews." Be sure students understand that the student doing the interviewing records the responses of the interviewee. Discuss interviewing etiquette and what is appropriate and inappropriate behavior during an interview. Interviewing and notetaking are often more successful when you send students out in pairs.

2. Give each student an additional copy (or copies) of Handout 1-9: "Peace Interviews" to use for homework. Have each student interview at least one person. You may want to assign (or solicit volunteers) to interview particular types of people, such as parents, older people, teenagers, etc.

3. When all the interviews are completed, give students an opportunity to share what they have found out. They might create a bulletin board display or bind the interview forms together to make a book.

4. As a variation, your students may prefer to develop a class interview form instead of using Handout 1-9. Small groups or individuals can develop interview questions, or the class can brainstorm a list of potential questions. From this they can select those questions they like best. They might "test out" the questions on each other before selecting the ones they want to use.

DISCUSSION QUESTIONS

- How did people react when you asked if you could interview them about peace?
- What answers did you like best? Why?
- Did people in particular groups have things in common?
- Did older people have answers that were different from those of younger people? Why or why not?
- Were there any surprises?

Handout 1-8
PEACE INTERVIEWS

My name: _____

My age: _____

I interviewed: _____

His/her age: _____

1. What are the first words or images you think of when you hear the word "peace"?

2. How do you define "peace"?

3. What are five things you do that make you feel peace?

4. What do you think a world at peace would be like?

5. What are some things you do that make the world more peaceful?

Don't forget to thank the person you interviewed!

9 PEACE PICTURES

GRADE LEVELS: K-6

OBJECTIVES: To make definitions of peace more complex; to explore how justice and injustice are related to peace

SUBJECT AREAS: Social studies

MATERIALS: Magazines, scissors, paste, paper, and two sets of ten pictures cut from magazines. The first set should be unambiguous pictures representing peace, such as people socializing, children playing without conflict, happy families, a beautiful country scene, etc. The second set should have mixed elements of peace and non-peace, such as a hungry child, a war scene, a polluting factory, etc.

INSTRUCTIONS

1. Show the first set of pictures one by one and have students describe what elements in each picture represent peace and/or a lack of peace.

2. Show the second set of pictures one by one and have students describe what aspects of each scene represent peace and/or a lack of peace.

3. Older students can select two (or find their own) pictures and write explanations of how each picture represents peace and the lack of peace.

4. Follow up the activity by having students make peace/nonpeace collages from magazine pictures. They can share these collages with the class and describe why they chose the pictures they did.

DISCUSSION QUESTIONS

- Did you add anything to your definition of peace as a result of this activity?
- If everything is calm and quiet, does that mean there is peace? Why or why not?
- What is the opposite of peace? If it is war, does that mean that when there is no war there is always peace?

10 WHAT PART IS PEACE?

GRADE LEVELS: 4-6

OBJECTIVES: To make definitions of peace more complex; to help students link the concept of peace to issues of justice

SUBJECT AREAS: Reading, language arts, social studies

MATERIALS: "Pieces of Peace" readings, Handout 1-10: "Looking for Pieces of Peace"

INSTRUCTIONS

1. Begin by using Activity 1-9: "Peace Pictures."

2. Read the following vignette aloud to the class:

Jerome is a second grader who was at an amusement park with his sister, who is in the fourth grade, and his brother, who is in the sixth. They were going to go on the roller coaster, but Jerome said, "I'm scared." His sister said, "What are you scared of?" Jerome said, "It's too high and too noisy and too fast." His brother said, "I used to be afraid of roller coasters until I rode on one with my friends. Then I learned it was fun."

"You don't have to go," said his sister. "But if you want to you can sit between us." "And you can close your eyes," said his brother. So Jerome gave it a try. He was terrified part of the time, but he felt safe between his brother and sister. When it was over they cheered him. "I want to go again!" he said.

3. Discuss the vignette using the questions on Handout 1-10: "Looking for Pieces of Peace." You may want to add some of the discussion questions below. You want to be sure that students grasp the idea that there are elements of peace and non-peace coexisting in the vignette.

4. Assign students to groups of three or four. Give each group a copy of Handout 1-10 and one of the "Pieces of Peace" readings. Have them read and discuss the vignettes and record their answers on the handout. Remind students that each group should be prepared to discuss what aspects of the vignette are peaceful and what aspects are not.

5. When groups have finished, you may have them respond to another vignette, or they may come together and discuss their responses with the whole class.

DISCUSSION QUESTIONS

- What could be done in this situation to bring out more of the peaceful elements?
- Have you ever been in a situation that had both elements of peace and non-peace? Tell about it.
- Can you think of a world situation that contains both elements of peace and non-peace?

GOING FURTHER

Have students write their own vignettes for discussion. Encourage them to include peaceful and nonpeaceful elements. Also, have students look for current events that contain both elements.

Reading
PIECES OF PEACE

Molly Haas is a 77-year-old woman. She lives alone. Her apartment is in an old building in a run-down part of town. Crime has been increasing in her neighborhood. She has placed bars on her windows and an extra lock on her door. Her home is a friendly and quiet place. She has friends who visit her. They drink tea and play cards. They listen to music and laugh. Molly has never been mugged or robbed, but many of her friends have been. She lives in constant fear for her safety.

■

Debbie Carr is a sixth grader. She was feeling sad after her class had had a discussion of current events. She had learned about thousands of children starving in countries like Ethiopia. She had heard about violence and war in Central America. After school Debbie took a walk in a big neighborhood park. She found a patch of soft grass underneath some big, shady trees and sat down. It was quiet in the park, and she relaxed. She forgot the problems that bothered her. She began to imagine that she was an elf princess in an enchanted forest. She stayed in the park under the shady trees until dinner time.

■

In a large company, the women workers are paid much less than the men. They do the same work. This was kept secret for a long time. But now the women workers know. They have threatened to take their case to court if the company doesn't give them equal pay. As a result of all the talk, things have changed. People are often angry with each other. There is a lot of complaining, arguing, and even yelling. Before anyone knew that women were paid less than men, it was a friendly place. People didn't argue.

■

Jamie and Andrew collect action figures. They like to play together after school. Sometimes they play at Jamie's house because he has all the G. I. Joe figures and equipment. Sometimes they play in Andrew's big back-yard. There they build battlefields for their figures. Together they set up the good guys and the bad guys. Then they act out violent battles. They make a lot of noise: shooting, explosions, and killing. For school, Andrew wrote a story about one of their most exciting battles. Jamie helped him draw a picture to illustrate the story. Their picture showed things exploding in bursts of bright orange flame.

■

Sharon's parents got a divorce last year. Her father moved to another city. Sharon misses him. She gets to see him only one weekend a month. But her father told her she can telephone him any time she wants. He also buys her a lot of presents. When he came to see her last month, he brought her two dolls with several outfits for each one. Then he took her out to a store and bought her a birthstone ring. He says he won't be able to see her at all next month, but that he will buy her a puppy and take her to Disney World next summer.

Handout 1-10
LOOKING FOR PIECES OF PEACE

1. Who is the main character in this story?

2. In what ways was this story peaceful?

3. In what ways was it not peaceful?

4. How do you think the main character felt in this story?

5. Did his or her feelings change? If so how?

Group Members: _____

‖ PEACE AND THE ENVIRONMENT

GRADE LEVELS: K-6

OBJECTIVES: To introduce environmental quality as an aspect of peace

SUBJECT AREAS: Science, social studies, thinking skills

MATERIALS: One or more of the following children's books:

Janet McCaffrey, *The Swamp Witch*. Fifinella the Swamp Witch has been careless with her environment, using so many frogs and insects in her mischievous potions that the living creatures are in danger of extinction. A terrified mole helps her turn her attention to creating potions that help people with their problems.

Edith Thatcher Hurd and Clement Hurd, *Wilson's World*.
This is the story of Wilson, who actually creates and empowers his own world, learning by his mistakes and changing his world when it becomes necessary.

Bill Peet, *The Wump World*. The Wumps, who love the land, are invaded by the Pollutians, whose disregard for the environment threatens to destroy it.

Dr. Seuss, *The Lorax*. The world where the Truffula trees grow is a peaceful place until the greedy Onceler chops down all the trees and builds polluting factories in order to make a profitable new product from the tufts of the trees. The visionary Lorax observes and deplores the violence done to the environment; the reader is left with the Lorax's haunting warning: "Unless . . . "

INSTRUCTIONS

1. Read any or all of the above books aloud to the children. Ask them to think about the following questions as they listen to the stories: What was the world like originally? What happened to change that world? What would you do if you were a character in the story to make the world right? What parts of the story illustrate peace and what parts illustrate the absence of peace? What message do you think the author is trying to convey to us?

DISCUSSION QUESTIONS

- What things in our environment do you especially enjoy or appreciate?
- In what ways is our environment in danger?
- What might we do to help this situation?
- What conditions in our world are similar to conditions in the stories?
- What other problems might occur in our world?
- How can people solve the existing problems?
- How might they help prevent additional problems?
- What might we do to help contribute to peace in the environment?

GOING FURTHER

You may want to follow this discussion with an action project that addresses an issue raised. This project might be as simple as picking up litter in the neighborhood or as challenging as participating in a recycling program. Helping children become involved in an action project gives them a sense of power to create a more peaceful world.

12 IT ISN'T FAIR!

GRADE LEVELS: K-6

OBJECTIVES: To relate justice to fairness; to explore fairness at personal, community, national, and international levels

SUBJECT AREAS: Social studies, thinking skills, language arts

MATERIALS: Chalkboard and chalk or newsprint and markers, 8½ x 11 paper, crayons

INSTRUCTIONS

1. Ask the children to share things they think are unfair; for example "It isn't fair when Jane talks to me and I'm the one who gets in trouble for talking"; "It isn't fair when I get a smaller serving of dessert than everyone else." Encourage them to share as long a list of specific, personal examples as they can. Write down all contributions on a list posted for all to see.

2. At some point the children will probably mention something unfair in the society rather than exclusively in their personal experience; for example, "It isn't fair when poor people don't have any money"; "It isn't fair that my uncle doesn't have a job." If this doesn't happen, guide their attention to social issues by such questions as: Can you think of something that doesn't seem fair for black people? For women? For people who live in (name of a place they are familiar with whose residents are protesting a local inequity)? How about something unfair in the story we read this morning? Something unfair you've seen on TV? Help the children extend their list to include as many examples of broader social unfairness as they can think of.

3. As a homework assignment, have the children "interview" adult friends and family members about what they think is unfair, and bring in the responses to add to the list. (This will not only extend the list of examples to include responses from a wider range of people, but may also help to carry your discussions of injustice into the children's homes.)

4. Make a book entitled "It Isn't Fair," in which each page is one of the examples on the list illustrated by a student. Each student can do several pages; the completed pages are then combined into a book. (During this stage of the activity, you might want to read aloud to the class *That Makes Me Mad!* by Stephen Kroll, a picture book similar in format to the book your class is making.) After their book is complete, read it aloud to the class, sharing the illustrations and again discussing the examples.

5. A variation on step 4 is to have students make "It Isn't Fair!" posters. These can be made on three-hole punched paper, so they can be displayed as posters or put into an "It Isn't Fair!" notebook.

DISCUSSION QUESTIONS

- Have you ever heard the expression "Life isn't fair?" What do you think it means? Why do people say it?
- People often have different points of view about what's fair and what isn't. Look over our list: what are some other points of view about the things that we said were unfair?

13 IF I WERE IN CHARGE

GRADE LEVELS: K-6

OBJECTIVES: To determine how unfair situations can be changed and made more fair; to develop imaginative solutions to problems; to relate working to correct injustice to peace

SUBJECT AREAS: Social studies, thinking skills, language arts

MATERIALS: "It Isn't Fair!" book from Activity 1-12: "It Isn't Fair!"

INSTRUCTIONS

1. Using the book "It Isn't Fair!" that your students created in the preceding activity, hold a group discussion around the question, "If you were in charge, what would you do to make these things *fair*?" Taking the examples one at a time, encourage the students to brainstorm remedies for the injustices. Help them go beyond the obvious, reality-based and superficial solutions to more detailed and imaginative ones. For example, in response to "It isn't fair when I get the smallest serving of dessert," the class might come up with "If I were in charge, every town would have a person in charge of serving desserts fairly. They would be specially trained in college and have to be elected to the job. If they gave some people more than others, they wouldn't get elected again. Every day at mealtime they would go around to the houses and serve the desserts."

2. With the more serious social issues, you will want to guide the discussion so that the suggestions aren't silly. Point out to the children that these are important problems many adults are working hard to solve. But do allow them to explore fanciful possibilities and come up with creative remedies. Remember, the goal is not for the children actually to cure the social ills, but rather to become aware of them as problems that need solutions and to think freely and imaginatively about what they would like to do.

3. Again have the children write and illustrate their "If I were in charge" statements on individual book pages. Each of these new pages should then be bound into the "It Isn't Fair!" book following the injustice it goes with, so that the final book balances each "It isn't fair!" statement with an "If I were in charge" solution to that problem.

4. Make a new cover for the book, changing the title to If I Were in Charge. Read it aloud again, sharing the pictures and discussing the ideas.

5. Throughout this activity, remind the students that they are exploring another aspect of peace–that peace is also being aware of things that aren't fair and doing something to make things better.

6. A variation on this activity is to have students work in groups of three. Each group chooses an "unfair situation" and brainstorms solutions to that problem.

DISCUSSION QUESTIONS

- What are some of the ways grown-ups try to make unfair things fair?
- Can you name some unfair things that have been made more fair?
- Who are some of the people who have tried to make things more fair?
- What happens when people disagree about how to make an unfair thing fair? Can you think of an example?

14 HUMAN NEEDS

GRADE LEVELS: (K-2), 3-6

OBJECTIVES: To distinguish between human needs and luxuries; to relate justice to meeting human needs

SUBJECT AREAS: Social studies, thinking skills

MATERIALS: 5 x 8 index cards, chalkboard and chalk, masking tape, or newsprint and markers

INSTRUCTIONS

1. Have the class brainstorm a list of things that the children feel are absolutely essential to survival; that is, without them people would die. Write each item on an index card, and display the cards on the chalkboard or bulletin board under the heading, "Essential." Encourage the children to exhaust their ideas for essential items even if they include a number of things that aren't strictly essential. (Basic needs that should be mentioned include air, food, water, clothing, and shelter; if any of these are overlooked, ask leading questions to elicit them.)

2. Introduce two additional categories, "Important But Not Essential," and "Nice Luxuries." Have the group consider each of the items they brainstormed as essential, applying the criterion that "people would die without this item." Move the cards among the categories, discussing and adding to the list, until the group agrees that the basic needs in the first category are air, food, water, clothing, and shelter. (Some might argue that basic medical care, contact with others, or other items should count as "essentials." Listen to their reasoning, and be flexible as you help them categories their ideas.)

3. Focus on the "Essential" list. Discuss: Do you have all these things? Does everyone you know have them? Do all the people in the world have them? Why or why not? What happens to people if one of these things is missing?

4. Next focus on the "Important But Not Essential" category. Go through the same list of questions used in step 3. Pay particular attention to the question: "Do all the people in the world have these items; why or why not?" Generate a list of reasons why not all people in the world have these items.

5. Focus on the "Luxuries" list. Again, go through the questions used in step 3. Point out (if a child doesn't do so) that fewer people have luxuries than have necessities. Raise the following questions: Why are these luxury items desirable? How do they improve the quality of life? Why do some people have more of them than others?

GOING FURTHER

Ask for volunteers to go without one of their favorite luxuries for a day, three days, or even a week. Students of mine have tried giving up such luxuries as candy, television, and Nintendo. (Be prepared, there's always someone who volunteers to give up school!) Have them keep a journal and report back their experiences to the class. This report should be an informal oral report in which they discuss how it felt, what was easy and difficult about the experience, how other people reacted, and whether or not they felt they were successful.

15 HUMAN RIGHTS AND RESPONSIBILITIES

GRADE LEVELS: (K-2), 3-6

OBJECTIVES: To introduce the concept of human rights and responsibilities; to relate rights and responsibilities to peace and justice

SUBJECT AREAS: Reading, social studies

MATERIALS: Newsprint and markers; Handout 1-15: "Our Civil Rights"; optional: copy of the Bill of Rights

INSTRUCTIONS

1. Begin by discussing the concept of rights. Ask: What are civil (or human) rights that you have in school? or What rights in other parts of your life? What do people mean when they say they have a "right" to do something?

2. Continue the discussion by having the class develop a list of civil rights for the classroom. List these on newsprint (save for later).

3. Distribute Handout 1-15: "Our Civil Rights." Read the handout with the class. Compare the list the class developed with the rights listed on the handout. Have the class make any changes they want to their own list. Ask for volunteers to make an "Our Civil Rights" poster for the class.

4. Explain that with rights come responsibilities. Discuss: What might be some of the responsibilities that go along with rights in our class? If students have trouble, ask: Responsibilities here at school? At home? In the community? Country? World? Record their answers on newsprint. Ask for another group of volunteers to make a poster called "Our Responsibilities."

5. Have students interview their parents about what they believe are the rights and responsibilities of citizens.

6. For younger students, simply read and discuss Handout 1-15: "Our Civil Rights." Ask students if they would add anything to it.

DISCUSSION QUESTIONS

- What is the Bill of Rights? What rights does it guarantee?
- How is the Bill of Rights similar to the handout on civil rights? How is it different?
- If there were a country where people did not have some of the rights we said were basic, in what ways would you say that country was peaceful? In what ways not peaceful? (Help students to more complex thinking about this question by pointing out that such a country might have a very low rate of violence. Elicit that violence is not always physical, and that without rights there is no justice; and justice, to many people, is an essential aspect of peace.)
- Are some rights more important or basic than others? If so, which ones?

GOING FURTHER

Introduce students to the United Nations document: "Declaration of the Rights of the Child." Compare it to Handout 1-15: "Our Civil Rights" and their own class list of rights. Older students can research and report on human rights watchdog organizations, such as Amnesty International and The Inter American Commission on Human Rights.

An excellent resource for teachers is *In the Child's Best Interest,* available from The Center for Peace and Conflict Studies, Wayne State University, Detroit, MI 48202.

"Our Civil Rights" is from Individual Differences: An Experience in Human Relations for Children by *Madison Public Schools, Madison, Wisc. Distributed by the Anti-Defamation League.*

Handout 1-15
OUR CIVIL RIGHTS

**I HAVE A RIGHT TO BE HAPPY AND TO BE
TREATED WITH COMPASSION IN THIS ROOM:**
THIS MEANS THAT NO ONE
WILL LAUGH AT ME
OR HURT MY FEELINGS.

I HAVE A RIGHT TO BE MYSELF IN THIS ROOM:
THIS MEANS THAT NO ONE WILL
TREAT ME UNFAIRLY BECAUSE I AM
BLACK OR WHITE,
FAT OR THIN,
TALL OR SHORT,
BOY OR GIRL.

I HAVE A RIGHT TO BE SAFE IN THIS ROOM:
THIS MEANS THAT NO ONE WILL
HIT ME,
KICK ME,
PUSH ME,
PINCH ME,
HURT ME.

I HAVE A RIGHT TO HEAR AND BE HEARD IN THIS ROOM:
THIS MEANS THAT NO ONE WILL
YELL,
SCREAM,
SHOUT,
OR MAKE LOUD NOISES.

I HAVE A RIGHT TO LEARN ABOUT MYSELF IN THIS ROOM:
THIS MEANS THAT I WILL BE
FREE TO EXPRESS MY FEELINGS
AND OPINIONS WITHOUT BEING
INTERRUPTED OR PUNISHED.

16 PEACE SYMBOLS

GRADE LEVELS: 1-6

OBJECTIVES: To interpret peace symbolically; to identify ways in which different people and cultures symbolize peace

SUBJECT AREAS: Social studies, art

MATERIALS: Picture of stop sign, international "No Smoking" sign, men's and women's room symbols, peace symbols (below)

**American
sign language**

**Dove with
olive branch**

**War resistor's
broken rifle**

**Italian
peace symbol**

Rainbow

**60s peace
sign**

**Mr. Spock's
hand signal
(Star Trek)**

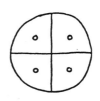

**Native American
earth sign**

INSTRUCTIONS

1. Discuss symbols. Hold up the stop sign and ask what it symbolizes. Ask: How did you learn what it means? Would you need to be able to read English to know what it means? (No. One reason people invent symbols is so important information can be conveyed even to those who cannot read.) Repeat with the "No Smoking" sign, and the men's and women's room signs. Discuss why an international symbol language has been developed.

2. Share some of the peace symbols. Ask if students know any others. Discuss the peace symbols. Let the children share what they may have learned about the origins and meanings of the symbols. Let them share also their personal reactions about them. Ask: Which do you respond to most strongly? Which most reflects the way peace feels to you?

3. Have the children design their own peace symbols. You might wish to have them reflect on their own personal times of peace, visualizing clearly the details of the situation, and then using some of the elements in creating their personal peace symbols. Share and display the designs.

DISCUSSION QUESTIONS

• Why do you think people make symbols representing peace?
• Why did you choose the symbol you did?
• Do you think other people will be able to understand it? Why?

GOING FURTHER

Students can make a quilt out of their peace symbols. These can be very simple. For example, each student can draw his or her symbol on a piece of 8½ x 11 paper. Tape all the class papers together to make a "quilt." For a more complex version, give each child a square of cloth on which to draw his or her symbol using fabric crayons or markers. Sew the patches together and hang the quilt on the wall.

17 PEACE IN OTHER LANGUAGES

GRADE LEVELS: K-6

OBJECTIVES: To introduce peace as an international concept

SUBJECT AREAS: Social studies

MATERIALS: Globe or world map

INSTRUCTIONS

1. Ask: Does anyone know how to say "peace" in another language? If there are any volunteers, have them teach the class how to say the word. Ask how they know that word.

2. Using the chart below, teach the class one new peace word each day.

Language	Word	Pronunciation
Latin	Pax	Pocks
Hebrew	Shalom	Shah-lohm
Italian	Pace	Pah-chay
Greek	Eirene	Ih-Ree-Nee
French	Paix	Peh
Arabic	Saalam	Sah-laahm
Vietnamese	Hoa-binn	Hwa-bean
German	Freden	Free-den
Japanese	Heciva	Hay-wah
Spanish	Paz	Poz (rhymes with nickname Roz)
Russian	Mir	Mear (rolled "r" at end)

Help younger children locate the country of origin on the globe or a world map. Older students may use foreign language dictionaries in the library and find the words themselves. They may also try to find synonyms for "peace" in that language.

3. Follow up this actiivity by using some of the international stories of peace referenced in chapter six, "Visions of Peace."

DISCUSSION QUESTIONS

- Why do you think so many languages have a word for peace?
- If you were learning another language, what other words would be useful to know?
- How might they be related to peace? (for example, hello, please, thank you, etc.)

18 THE WORLD CITIZEN SONG

GRADE LEVELS: (2-3), 4-6

OBJECTIVES: To introduce the concept of world citizenship through a song

SUBJECT AREAS: Social studies, music

MATERIALS: Handout 1-18: "World Citizen Song"

INSTRUCTIONS

1. Distribute Handout 1-18: "World Citizen Song." Sing the song together several times until students are comfortable with it. Once the class has mastered the song, there are several possible activities.

2. "World Citizen" can be used as a rousing beginning to a concert of songs from around the world or songs about peace.

3. The lyrics to "World Citizen" offer a rich starting point for discussion. You might begin by having students locate the cities named in verses one and two. Several important peace-related concepts are introduced in verses two, three, and four: interconnectedness, the importance of conflict resolution, appreciating diversity, working together, and the importance of individual actions. Students may also think of additions to the third and fourth lines of the chorus, and discuss the last line.

4. Finally, there are several assumptions in the song. Is everyone able to "pick up a phone" or "get on a plane?" This can be a starting point for discussing some inequities among the world's citizens.

Handout 1-18
WORLD CITIZEN SONG

To the tune of "The Wabash Cannonball"

From Timbuktu to Lima Peru
From Shanghai to Nepal
From the Kremlin Wall in Moskva
To the ancient China wall
From Tyrol to Vladivostock
From Cairo to Capetown
From Sydney to Seattle
I've got neighbors the whole world round.

Chorus:
I'm a world citizen (world citizen)
Step up 'n shake my hand.
I'm not just from _____Carolina/Odessa/Novosibirsk/ The USSR
I'm not just _____ American/ Ukranian/ Siberian/ American
I'm a world citizen (world citizen)
Home the whole world round.
You and I can break those borders down!

(You and I can break those borders down!!)

You can pick up a phone almost anywhere
And call up Singapore.
And you can get on a plane in Myorda, Spain
And fly to El Salvador
The world keeps gettin' smaller,
And we keep gettin' strong.
But we're not gettin' anywhere
If we don't get along!

There's always confrontation,
We just might disagree.
You can be a world citizen,
And not think just like me!
We're all ridin' on the same train
With a lot of work to do.
But no one's just a passenger–
Everyone's part of the crew!

People all around the world
Lookin' for peace to come.
We're every shade of the rainbow
We're big and little ones.
We're joinin' hands together,
Our voices sound out strong.
Help us build a peaceful world
And help us sing this song!

Written by Stuart Stotts
(Rusty Rose Music, 169 Ohio Avenue, Madison, WI 53704)

Chapter Two:
PEACE AND COMMUNITY BUILDING

INTRODUCTION

Peace doesn't just happen magically. There are things that help it happen–things like working together to solve problems, communicating clearly, helping and caring for others, and appreciating diversity. These are all contributing factors in creating peace.

To some extent, all of these things have skill components. They can be taught, practiced, and used. They are also norms and values that have been acknowledged, if not practiced, for a long time. Put together, they are my definition of a caring community. In my book *Creative Conflict Resolution* I called it "the peaceable classroom." It has five qualities: cooperation, communication, emotional expression, appreciation for diversity, and conflict resolution. Since developing that model, I have added more emphasis on caring as an essential part of the peaceable classroom.

I don't believe that this concept of a caring community can be separated from peace if peace is to be a bold and dynamic concept. It is in such a context of community, whether it is the family, the classroom, the school, the church, or some other institution, that children have their first experiences with peace. And it is in the context of community that they best learn about such things as cooperation and how to value diversity. They learn about them by being taught the appropriate skills and practicing them in a context where those skills are valued and appreciated.

This chapter has four sections. The activities in section one (numbers 1-4) deal with defining the nature of community. Section two (numbers 5-11) helps students learn to cooperate and work together effectively. Section three (numbers 12-15) deals with caring communication. Section four (numbers 16-20) concerns global community. Other aspects of community building, such as appreciating diversity and dealing with conflict, are dealt with in later chapters.

Note: Activities in this chapter use the term "peaceable," the adjectival form of peace, meaning "fond of, inclined toward, or promoting peace." You will need to explain the term to children.

Teaching Considerations

Stay concrete and specific. Community is a broad and somewhat vague concept, but it is comprised of specific skills and behaviors, such as cooperation, caring communication, and being supportive. Emphasize them when you talk with students about community.

• Give students a few minutes at the end of each activity to reflect on how well they are doing and how they might improve. Building community is an intentional process, and students need to think about the skills they are acquiring. Nancy and Ted Graves recommend the IAG format: Identify, Analyze, Generalize.

Identify—"what":

- What social skills did you see or hear during the activity?
- What happened in our community today?
- What did you feel when it happened?

Analyze—"why" and "how":

- Why do you think that happened?
- How could it happen differently next time?
- How did you solve problems in your group?

Generalize—"when" and "where":

- When could we use such and such a skill?
- Where are other problems occurring that we could work on?
- When do people in our town (or state or country) have a similar problem?

This reflection can take place as a class or in small groups. It can be written or oral. It is useful for you to add your feedback to the discussion, but the emphasis should be on the children identifying and discussing their own behavior. Your questions help guide students, though, and many of the activities in this chapter contain questions to facilitate reflection.

After they have reflected on their progress, help students set goals and plans for improvement. These can be both class goals ("We will keep the area by the sink clean and dry and this is how . . . ") and individual ones ("I will be more encouraging of other people and this is how . . .").

The activities in this chapter are not intended as a guide to cooperative learning. I recommend that the teacher who is interested in building community in her or his classroom look into cooperative learning. Several excellent resources are listed in Appendix C.

Connecting to Larger Issues

Every personal experience of community has an analogy at other levels: local community, state, national, and international. From time to time ask students to compare what they are doing in the classroom with what happens on another level: How do adults do something similar to what you are doing? How does this happen in our town? When does this happen between countries?

• Most of the daily tasks in our classrooms are performed in one way or another by children around the world. Build on these. For example, if you are teaching handwriting, ask: How is handwriting taught in Japan? Or Bolivia? Find out what your students know, then help them gather more information. Such questions need not take a lot of time, and they do motivate children to learn about other cultures. They are also fun. Another approach is for you to dig up interesting facts for the children to explore. Try this one during spelling: In Russia, students don't have any spelling classes. Why? It's an instant attention getter!

WHAT WOULD A PEACEABLE CLASSROOM BE LIKE?

GRADE LEVELS: K-6

OBJECTIVES: To identify qualities of community in a classroom; to make the connection between peace and community

SUBJECT AREAS: *None*

MATERIALS: Chalkboard and chalk or chart paper and markers

INSTRUCTIONS

1. Remind students of some of the ideas they had when the defined "peace." Ask: What would a peaceable classroom be like"? Emphasize that you do not mean peaceable as in quiet, or restful but as actively promoting a dynamic peace. (You may need to explain that "peaceable" means fond of or inclined toward or promoting peace.)

2. Have the class brainstorm a list of qualities that characterize a peaceable classroom. Students will tend to respond with very specific qualities. Elicit such attributes as: cooperative, good communication, respect for one another, nonviolent conflict resolution, problem solving. If their responses are too general–"everyone is nice"–encourage them to be more specific.

3. Introduce the term "community." Ask students for a definition and examples of community. Explain that a peaceable classroom is a caring community.

DISCUSSION QUESTIONS

- If this is what a peaceable classroom looks like, how does our classroom compare? Do we have a peaceable classroom? Is our classroom a caring community?
- What would we have to do to get a peaceable classroom?
- What are some caring communities you are a part of? In what ways do they resemble our peaceable classroom?

GOING FURTHER

Have students identify one quality of a peaceable classroom that they feel they need to work on as a class. Examples are: not calling names, working together more harmoniously, being more respectful of community property.

Make this the "Peaceable Classroom Goal" of the week. Have students brainstorm ways to meet this goal in the coming week and come up with a way they might assess their progress at the end of the week. This gives the class a chance to identify, take ownership of, and solve specific community building problems.

2 YOU'RE THE TEACHER

GRADE LEVELS: 2-6

OBJECTIVES: To identify community-building behaviors in specific situations

SUBJECT AREAS: Language arts, drama

MATERIALS: None

INSTRUCTIONS

1. This is a simple and fun discussion activity. It can be done as a structured lesson or at odd moments when you want to engage the children. It also provides opportunity for you to gain some interesting insights into how your students view your role in the class.

2. Have students pretend that they are the teachers in a peaceable classroom. As teachers they are responsible for dealing with certain types of situations, but as teachers in a peaceable classroom they want to do so in a way that builds community, that encourages students to make decisions, and that encourages a sense of belonging and caring.

3. Ask what they, as teachers, would do in one of the following situations:

• A new child who doesn't speak any English arrives in the class.
• The students in the class fight a lot.
• One class member was sick and was out for four months.
• One child never wants to share.
• The class always excludes a particular boy or girl.
• The girls and the boys never want to work together.
• One child is a real bully.
• A boy or girl constantly calls other students names.

DISCUSSION QUESTIONS

• What do you think are some of the hard decisions a teacher has to make?
• What do you think are some of the fun parts of being a teacher?
• A teacher can't create a peaceable classroom all by him or herself. What are some of the ways the students help?

3 INTERVIEWING COMMUNITY BUILDERS

GRADE LEVELS: 1-6

OBJECTIVES: To interview people who contribute positively to the community; to identify community-building behavior

SUBJECT AREAS: Social studies, language arts

MATERIALS: 3 x 5 cards, resource people

INSTRUCTIONS

1. Invite someone from the community to come to the classroom to be interviewed by the students on the subject of "Contributing to a peaceable community." The range of possible invitees is endless. Some that I've tried are a mediator, the mayor, superintendent of schools, visiting nurse, lawyer, police officer, librarian, waitress, cashier, various volunteer workers, and a professional umpire.

2. Prior to the visit, explain the person's background to the class. Give each student a 3 x 5 card on which to write a question to ask the visitor. Review the cards to see if the students are on track in the types of questions they ask. Possible questions are: How did you get started in your activity? How do you see it helping to make a peaceable community? What do you think peace is? Did you ever have to make a tough decision?

3. Have students write thank you notes in which they mention something they learned from the visit and thank the guest both for the visit and the work he or she does.

4. Repeat the activity throughout the year. You may want to ask several people to come at one time, or you might have one person a month. Try to get a variety of people so students can see the wide range of ways an individual can contribute to the community.

DISCUSSION QUESTIONS

- Did you learn anything from this person that surprised you?
- What ideas did you get for community building?
- If we asked this person back, is there another question you'd like to ask him or her?
- Are there things this grown-up does that you could do in school to contribute to a peaceful community?

Adapted from Perspectives at Work: Fourteen Activities for Building Peacemaking Skills *by Sarah Pirtle. Traprock Peace Center, Woolman Hill, Deerfield, MA 01342, p. 4-5.*

4 2010: The Space Station Community

GRADE LEVELS: 4-6

OBJECTIVES: To identify aspects of community building by designing a space community

MATERIALS: Paper and crayons

INSTRUCTIONS

1. Divide students into groups. Explain that each group's task is to design an extraterrestrial colony located in space (or, if you prefer, on another planet). The inhabitants will be representatives of each populated continent.

2. Group members will need to discuss and decide some or all of the following:

- What will be the purpose of the colony?
- Who will go? How many? From where? How will they be chosen?
- How will they get to the colony? What jobs will they perform?
- How will the colony look? What structures and dwellings will be needed? What purposes will the structures serve?
- How will inhabitants obtain food? What, if anything, will they manufacture? How will they trade? What money will they use?
- How will cultural differences affect the colony? How will the inhabitants make it a community?
- How will it be governed? What recreation will there be? What kind of communication?

3. Have each group write a report of the colony in which the students answer the questions above. They may also illustrate the report with drawings of various aspects of colony life.

DISCUSSION QUESTIONS

- What did you do well as a group?
- What could you do better next time?
- What did you learn about community building?
- What were the most difficult problems for the space community? How were they like problems on earth? How were they different?

GOING FURTHER

Students can write letters home about life in the multicultural space community. Students who wish to learn more about space stations should look for Franklyn M. Branley. *Space Colony: Frontier of the Twenty First Century* (Elsevier/Dutton, 1982) or Frederic Golden. *Colonies in Space: The Next Giant Step* (Harcourt, Brace, Jovanovitch, 1977).

Adapted from Worldways, Bring the World into the Classroom by Pamela Elder and Mary Ann Carr. Copyright 1987, Addison-Wesley Publishing Company, Menlo Park, California.

5 RAINSTORM

GRADE LEVELS: K-6

OBJECTIVES: To experience cooperation by playing a game; to simulate the sound of a rainstorm

SUBJECT AREAS: Physical education

MATERIALS: None

INSTRUCTIONS

1. Have students sit in a circle. Explain that the object of the game is to simulate the sound of a rainstorm.

2. For younger children, have the leader stand inside the circle and move around the circle, stopping in front of each child. As the leader moves around the circle, she or he makes the following movements or sounds, and the others imitate the movement: (1) rubbing hands together; (2) snapping fingers; (3) slapping legs with hands; and, at the height of the storm, (4) stamping feet. Reverse the movements until the storm subsides. (The first time you play the game you should probably be the leader yourself.)

3. For older students, begin by rubbing your hands together and passing that movement to the student on your right, who then passes it to the student on her right, and so on around the circle until all the students are rubbing their hands together. Begin snapping your fingers and pass that movement to the student on your right, who then passes it to the student on her right, and so on. Continue with slapping legs with palms of hands and then slapping legs and stamping feet simultaneously. This is the height of the storm. Reverse the order as the storm subsides.

DISCUSSION QUESTIONS

- How did it feel to make a "rainstorm"?
- In this activity you did something together you could not have done alone. What are some other activities you cannot do without other people?

6 FROZEN BEANBAG

GRADE LEVELS: K-2

OBJECTIVES: To experience cooperation by playing a game; to experience helping others as a part of cooperation

SUBJECT AREAS: Social skills

MATERIALS: One beanbag for each child

INSTRUCTIONS

1. Explain that the object of this game is for children to help each other so that everyone can keep moving as long as possible.

2. Give each child a beanbag to put on his or her head. Each child should move around the room or designated play area.

3. If the beanbag slips off a child's head, he or she is "frozen" and must stop moving. Children who see someone frozen should try to help that person by picking up the beanbag and replacing it on the frozen child's head. If the helper's beanbag should fall off during this, then she or he is frozen as well. Soon everyone will be frozen.

DISCUSSION QUESTIONS

• What things helped you keep the beanbag on your head?
• How can you ask for help when you need it?
• What are some of the ways you help people in our classroom?

GOING FURTHER

For more cooperative games, see Appendix C, Curricula and Other Resources for Teachers.

7 GROUP CLAY SCULPTURES

GRADE LEVELS: K-6

OBJECTIVES: To create a group sculpture out of clay; to identify some of the benefits of working in groups

SUBJECT AREAS: Art

MATERIALS: Clay (enough for each student to have an apple-sized piece)

INSTRUCTIONS

1. Pass out a ball of playdough or clay about the size of an apple. Tell the children they are going to make three shapes: a ball, a cube, and a snake. They can make them any size or way, but they have to use all of the playdough or clay. Once all the children are finished, they will put all of the pieces together to make a group sculpture.

2. Use large colored paper as a background for the group sculpture.

3. Explain that to make a group sculpture out of the balls, cubes, and snakes, one person at a time will place a shape on the sculpture. There is no talking. They can put any piece on in any order they want.

4. Once all the pieces are in place, have everyone walk around the sculpture to look at it from many positions: eye level, from the floor, sitting, standing, and stooping down. Have students pick their favorite part of the sculpture and explain what they like about it.

DISCUSSION QUESTIONS

• What was it like to be the *first* person to place a piece (or the last)?
• How did it feel to have someone put a piece where you wanted something different?
• What parts surprised you as the sculpture grew?
• How is it different from a sculpture you might have made working all alone or with only one or two other friends?
• Decide as a group what is to be done with the sculpture. Do people want to squash it, punch it down, take care of it by taking it down piece by piece? Or do they want to put it on display somewhere in the school with an explanation of how it was built?

8 SQUIGGLE DRAWING

GRADE LEVELS: K-6

OBJECTIVES: To create a group drawing; to identify some of the problems that arise in groups; to identify solutions to those problems

SUBJECT AREAS: Art, social skills

MATERIALS: Drawing paper (18 x 24 or larger), crayons

INSTRUCTIONS

1. Divide students into groups of four or five. Give each group an identical sheet of large (18 x 24 or bigger) drawing paper with a "squiggle" drawn on it in black felt pen. Also include a set of lines on which they will later write their names. At this point each group's paper is the same as all the others.

2. Each group goes to a separate area of the room so the groups can't overhear each other, and the students brainstorm ideas for what the "squiggle" might be turned into. Encourage them to turn the paper in each of the four directions to look at. Go from group to group and help draw out the students' ideas. Ask if *everyone* is sharing ideas and encourage them to help draw out a more quiet group member; praise cooperative behavior you observe and model it wherever you can. Help each group add more details to its ideas for the squiggles. Instruct the students to agree upon what they as a group want to turn their squiggle into.

3. When all groups have their ideas, distribute one crayon to each student, giving each child in a group a different color. The children may use *only* the crayon they were given so that each color will represent the work of a single child. Instruct the children to write their names on the paper using their color crayon.

4. Next, each group adds to its squiggle to complete the picture it decided upon. The group decides what to draw where, and the actual drawing is done by the child whose crayon is the appropriate color. (It will be easy to see who does most of the drawing by the predominance of the child's color.) Encourage the groups to add final details and write a good title for their drawing.

5. Bring groups back together to share their drawings. All the children should be given the opportunity to comment on their group's drawing. Give each group enough time to comment on its drawing before going to the discussion on group process.

DISCUSSION QUESTIONS

- What can we tell from the colors of the drawings about sharing the task and whether everyone got a turn?
- Did anyone feel left out?
- Did someone in your group do something to help others?
- What difficulties arose, and who did something to smooth out the difficulty?
- What made the task harder? What made it easier? (Encourage children to acknowledge specific, helpful things others did.)

GOING FURTHER

Repeat the activity a week or so later–with a different "squiggle" but without changing the rest of the format of the activity–to give the children an opportunity to build on what they've learned about cooperation.

As an additional follow-up, let the children write stories based on the squiggle picture done by their group. They can do this as a cooperative group effort or individually, depending upon whether or not you perceive a need for the group process to be balanced by a time for individual creativity.

9 WHAT'S YOUR ROLE?

GRADE LEVELS: (K-1), 2-6

OBJECTIVES: To identify the roles students can play in groups; to identify how those roles can facilitate the group's work

SUBJECT AREAS: Social skills

MATERIALS: Signs made of 8½ x 11 paper that say: Resource Person, Recorder, Facilitator, Spokesperson

INSTRUCTIONS

1. One of the most common problems students have when they work in groups is inclusion/exclusion. This can take the form of the child who is left out, the bossy child, the child who can't get a word in edgewise, and so on. Assigning roles in the group is one way to deal with this problem. When everyone has a role, it's harder for any one person to be left out and for anyone to take over.

Note: Assigning roles usually reduces the problems of inclusion/exclusion, but it will probably not eliminate them. You will still need to monitor groups.

2. There are many possible roles in groups. Four that work well for elementary children are:

• Resource person: collects materials
• Recorder: writes down anything that needs to be written
• Facilitator: makes sure everyone gets a turn, asks questions
• Spokesperson: reports to the class

3. Give students a chance to try these roles in the cooperative activities suggested in this book, such as 2-8: "Squiggle Drawing" or 2-4: "2010:The Space Station Community."

DISCUSSION QUESTIONS

- Did having roles help your group work together?
- What did you like about your role?
- What was difficult about your role?
- What skills do you need to practice to get better at your role?
- What are some other roles people might play in groups?
- What are some roles that don't help a group work together?

10 THE 100 CARAT TEAM NAME

GRADE LEVELS: 4-6

OBJECTIVES: To cooperatively create a team name with letters that add up to 100 carats; to build community and cooperative skills

SUBJECT AREAS: Cooperation skills, communication skills

MATERIALS: Paper and pencil, crayons, or markers

INSTRUCTIONS

1. Divide students into groups of four. Extra members can from a group of three or five. Explain that a "carat" is a unit of weight used for gems.

2. Pose a simple preliminary exercise: If the letter A has a weight of 1 carat, B equals 2 carats and C equals 3 carats, and so on, what is the weight of your first name? When everyone in your group has figured this out, raise your hands. Who in your group has the heaviest name? The lightest name?

3. Assign the roles of spokesperson and recorder to the students with the lightest and heaviest names.

4. Explain the group task: In ten minutes come up with a team name in which all the letters add up to 100 carats. The name can be one or more words, and nonsense words are okay as long as you all agree that is what you want for your team name.

5. When each group is finished, it may make a poster with its team name and share it with the class.

6. As a variation, have groups develop three or five-hundred carat names.

DISCUSSION QUESTIONS

• Did everyone in your group have a chance to contribute?
• What things did you do to encourage everyone to contribute?
• How did your group make sure everyone was satisfied with the team name?
• If you weren't able to finish in ten minutes, what could you do differently next time?

GOING FURTHER

Have students calculate the weight of their first names, and then line up from lightest to heaviest.

This activity was suggested by Bethel Smith of the Brookline (Mass.) school system.

PRACTICING GROUP DECISION MAKING

GRADE LEVELS: (K-2), 3-6

OBJECTIVES: To introduce group decision-making procedures; to provide structured practice in group decision making

SUBJECT AREAS: Social skills

MATERIALS: Handout 2-11: "Group Decision-Making Strategies"

INSTRUCTIONS

1. Divide students into groups of four. Designate a spokesperson for each group. Explain to the groups: Your group has just won an all-expenses paid two-week vacation anywhere in the world. Your task as a group is to decide on the one place where you will take all your vacation together.

2. Explain that they will have 15-20 minutes to discuss the possibilities and come to a decision. If they fail to come to a decision, they will lose their prize.

3. When the time is up, have the spokesperson report the group's decision, if any, and the method(s) used to arrive at that decision. List these methods on the board. When all the groups have reported, review the list with the class. If anyone can identify any decision-making strategies not listed, add them to the list. Discuss the advantages and disadvantages of each method.

4. Distribute Handout 2-11: "Group Decision-Making Strategies." Read the handout with the class and compare it with the strategies listed on the board.

5. Extend this activity by repeating it. This time the challenge should be: The group has just won a $5,000 prize in a lottery. But the group must agree on one prize that all the members will share. What should it be? Have the groups choose a decision-making strategy from the handout.

6. For younger students, introduce one decision-making strategy at a time and give them a problem on which to practice that strategy. Some good problem situations are choosing a field trip, a group pet, or a group toy.

DISCUSSION QUESTIONS

- When might you want to make a decision by voting? By consensus? Compromise? Etc.
- What is an experience you had using one of the decision-making strategies on the handout? (or: What is an experience you had with voting? or consensus?) How did it work out?
- What does a group need to think about before it chooses a decision-making strategy? (For example, How important is the decision? How much time is there? What will the consequences be if some people in the group dislike the decision?)

Adapted from What is Cooperative Learning? Tips for Teachers and Trainers *by Nancy and Ted Graves. Cooperative College of California, 136 Liberty St., Santa Cruz, CA 95060, p. 4.5*

Handout 2-11
GROUP DECISION-MAKING STRATEGIES

The Leader Decides

The group chooses a leader. The leader hears what everyone thinks. Then the leader decides what the group will do.

Chance Decides

The group flips a coin or draws straws to choose what it will do.

Consensus Decision

Everyone in the group agrees on one choice or solution. The group does not vote. The group members listen to each other. Then they come to an agreement on a common solution.

Compromise Decision

Everybody in the group agrees to give up a little of what they want . They try to find a solution everyone can accept.

Voting Decision

Several choices or solutions are suggested. Group members say which one they like. The choice most people like is the one the group chooses.

Expert Decision

The person in the group who is an "expert" or knows the most about the problem makes the decision.

Arbitration Decision

The group asks an outsider to make a decision for them. The outsider is called the arbitrator. The group agrees to do what she or he decides.

12 GREEN POISON DARTS

GRADE LEVELS: K-6

OBJECTIVES: To identify put-downs; to determine why put-downs are a problem for communities

SUBJECT AREAS: Social skills

MATERIALS: Chart paper with seven circles drawn on it; green crayon or marker; "Green Poison Darts" story

INSTRUCTIONS

Note: This activity uses the term "put-down." Your students may use another term, *such as* "capping."

1. Ask: What's a put-down? Elicit: insulting or hurtful remarks, name-calling, etc. How does it feel to be put-down? Why do people put others down?

2. Explain: Put-downs form a special problem for a caring community. They spread throughout a community and destroy peace.

3. Post the chart paper and tell the following story. At the appropriate points in the story, draw lines from one circle to another and color the circle green.

One day Roger (point to one of the circles) was having a lot of trouble with his math. He was getting really frustrated, and he started putting himself down. "I'm so stupid," he said to himself. "I never get anything right." He was so mad at himself it was as if he filled up with a green poison (color in the circle). Maria, who sat next to him (point to a circle) asked, "Hey Roger, can I borrow a pencil?"

"Shut your fat mouth," Roger said. "I'm trying to work." It was as if he shot a poison dart at Maria (draw a line from Roger to Maria). Maria felt hurt, and she felt like she was filled with green poison (color in the Maria circle). "You shut up," she said.

Tanesha came up to Maria. "Can you help me with this spelling?" she asked. Maria shot a green poison dart at Tanesha. "You're so stupid you always need help," she said (draw a line from Maria to Tanesha). "Do it yourself." "You're the stupid one," said Tanesha. She filled up with green poison herself.

Tanesha sat down. Two boys near her were talking to each other. Tanesha shot green poison darts at them. They filled up with green poison and then shot green poison darts at people by putting them down and calling names. Soon the whole class was filled with green poison and was shooting green poison darts at each other over and over.

DISCUSSION QUESTIONS

- What's the difference between put-downs and good-natured teasing?
- What can you do if you're feeling mad besides put someone down?
- Have you ever felt like you were filled with green poison? What can you do when you feel that way?
- What can you do when someone else puts you down so that you don't fill up with green poison?

GOING FURTHER

Have students identify a positive alternative to "Green Poison Darts." One class of mine developed "Warm Orange Goop" as their metaphor for spreading good feelings through the room.

13 WHAT'S IN A NAME?

GRADE LEVELS: 4-6

OBJECTIVES: To encourage personal sharing about names; to decrease name-calling by fostering mutual respect

SUBJECT AREAS: Language arts, social studies

MATERIALS: None

INSTRUCTIONS

1. Assign students to pairs. If possible, pair students with someone they don't know well.

2. Explain that they will each have five minutes to tell their partner about their name.

• What do you know about the meaning of your name?
• Who gave you your name, and why did they choose it?
• How do you feel about your name?
• What do you know about your family name, or middle name?
• Would you like to be called by a nickname or some other name?

It is helpful to model this by taking a few minutes to talk with the class about your name.

3. Encourage students to practice good listening skills, and tell them that they should be prepared to tell the class one thing they learned about their partner's name.

4. When both people have had a chance to share, bring the class together and quickly have every student tell one thing they learned about their partner's name. Or have each pair join with another pair into a group of four, in which the students can each share one thing they learned about their partner's name.

DISCUSSION QUESTIONS

• What did your partner do as a listener that helped you to talk?
• What did you do as a listener that was helpful?
• What might you do better next time?

Adapted from What is Cooperative Learning? Tips for Teachers and Trainers *by Nancy and Ted Graves. Cooperative College of California, 136 Liberty St., Santa Cruz, CA 95060, p. 3.43.*

14 ENCOURAGING ENCOURAGEMENT

GRADE LEVELS: 2-6

OBJECTIVES: To practice the skill of encouragement; to identify the behavioral components of encouragement

SUBJECT AREAS: Language arts

MATERIALS: Paper and crayons

INSTRUCTIONS

1. Ask the class: What is encouragement? What does it mean to be encouraging? Was there a time when someone was encouraging to you? After discussing encouragement in general terms, ask students to be more specific and list their contributions on the board in four categories:

- What does encouragement look like? What expressions do people have on their faces?
- What does encouragement sound like? What kinds of things do people say when they are being encouraging?
- What doesn't encouragement look like?
- What are not encouraging things to say?

2. Divide the class into groups of three or four. Explain that their task is to design an invention that will help clean up the environment. They will have twenty minutes to draw a picture of their invention and write a short description telling how it works. Assign roles: materials person, recorder, checker, and spokesperson. Explain that there are only two rules:

- Everyone in the group helps to decide what the invention is like.
- Everyone in the group helps draw the invention.

3. Emphasize that as students work on their inventions they should focus on being encouraging. The goal of this activity is to practice being encouraging.

4. When the groups have finished, have them share their inventions. Follow this with discussion and reflection on how well the groups did at being encouraging. Give your own feedback to the group generally and to individuals. **Note:** if students had a hard time being encouraging, point out what they did well and explain that they will have other chances to practice.

DISCUSSION QUESTIONS

- In what ways were you encouraging to the people in your group?
- In what ways were they encouraging to you?
- How could you or they have been more encouraging?
- What problems did you have being encouraging? What did you do for example, when someone suggested an idea you thought was really dumb?
- Would you add anything to our lists of what encouragement is?

GOING FURTHER

This model can be used to pinpoint and practice any number of social skills, not just encouragement. The key is to be very specific about what the skill does and does not look and sound like. Follow up with a chance to practice the skill, and then reflect and give feedback on the activity.

15 CREATURE FEATURE

GRADE LEVELS: 3-6

OBJECTIVES: To experience differences in communication styles; to see how differing communication styles affect interactions between people.

DURATION: Two class periods, each of approximately thirty minutes

MATERIALS: Crayons or colored pencils, Handout 2-15: Planets

INSTRUCTIONS: Class Period 1

1. Discuss with students what is meant by the term "communication style" in the following passage.

When we listen to other people, we notice the words they say. But we also notice *how* they say the words. Some people speak loudly; others speak softly, . Some people move their hands; others stand very still. Each person has a different way of talking, and this is called our "communication style." If two people have very different communication styles, one person may have a lot of trouble understanding the other person, even though they both speak the same language.

2. Explain to students that they will work in groups, and that each group will be from a different imaginary planet. Each planet is inhabited by an imaginary creature that has a particular communication style.

3. Divide students into five groups. Give each group one of the "Planet" sections of the handout.

4. Review privately with each group the description of the creature from its planet. Make sure that the students understand the mechanics of their creature's communication style. (If possible, they might practice talking with one another using the communication style of their creature. However, this should be done out of sight or hearing of the other small groups.)

5. Ask the members of each group to work together to complete the questions on its own "Planet" handout, and to draw a picture of its creature. Collect the five pictures (one from each group) and display them at the front of the class. (Do not display completed handouts, however.)

6. Explain that tomorrow will be an interplanetary visiting day, and that creatures from each planet will visit other planets to get to know one another. Instruct "planet" groups NOT to discuss their planets or creatures with students from other planets.

INSTRUCTIONS: Class Period 2

7. Put students in their small groups, and briefly review again with each group the mechanics of its creature's communication style.

8. Select two students from Planet 1 and two students from Planet 2. Ask them to come to the front of the class and start a conversation with the students from the other planet. Each pair should try to find out from the other the answers to questions 1, 3, and 4 on the "Planet" handout (What is the name of your planet? What is the weather like on your planet? What do you eat?)

Note: Instruct students to demonstrate the communication style of their creature during the discussion. For example, the students from Planet 1 will speak very softly and attempt to stand close to the students from Planet 2, while those from Planet 2 will attempt to move far away.

9. After a few minutes, stop the conversation and discuss the following questions with the class.

• What happened?
• How would you describe the communication style of each kind of creature?
• What made it difficult for the creatures to communicate? What made it easy?

10. Repeat steps 8 and 9 as often as time allows, selecting pairs of students in the following combinations:

Planet 3 and Planet 5
Planet 4 and Planet 5
Planet 2 and Planet 3
Planet 1 and Planet 4

DISCUSSION QUESTIONS

- What are some communication styles we use? What are some differences in the ways people communicate?
- How does our communication style affect the conversations we have with other people?
- If people have different communication styles, what can they do to make it easier to talk with one another?
- Can you think of a time when you had trouble communicating with someone who had a different communication style from yours? What happened?
- How might differing communications styles lead to conflict or make a conflict worse? Can you think of an example?

From Conflict Resolution in the Elementary Classroom *by Gail Sadalla, Meg Holmberg, Jim Halligan. The Community Board Program, 149 Ninth St., San Francisco, CA 94103, pp. 4-53-4-60.*

Handout 2-15
PLANETS

Planet 1

The creatures from your planet speak softly and feel highly insulted if they are asked to repeat anything. In order to hear well, they stand very close to the person they're talking to.

Please work together as a group to answer the following questions:

1. What is the name of your planet?

2. What does your creature look like?
(Please draw a picture on a separate piece of paper)

3. What is the weather like on your planet?

4. What does your creature eat?

5. What is the best thing about the way your creature communicates?

6. What is the hardest thing about the way your creature communicates?

7. Practice communicating the way creatures on your planet communicate.

Planet 2

The creatures from your planet illustrate everything they say with enormous hand and arm gestures. In order to have enough room to do this, they stand very far apart when talking (about 8 to 10 feet away from the person they're talking to.)

Please work together as a group to answer the following questions:

1. What is the name of your planet?

2. What does your creature look like?
(Please draw a picture on a separate piece of paper)

3. What is the weather like on your planet?

4. What does your creature eat?

5. What is the best thing about the way your creature communicates?

6. What is the hardest thing about the way your creature communicates?

7. Practice communicating the way creatures on your planet communicate.

Planet 3

The creatures from your planet can communicate only when their backs are touching. Before they begin speaking, they must turn so that their back touches the other person's back.

Please work together as a group to answer the following questions:

1. What is the name of your planet?

2. What does your creature look like?
(Please draw a picture on a separate piece of paper)

3. What is the weather like on your planet?

4. What does your creature eat?

5. What is the best thing about the way your creature communicates?

6. What is the hardest thing about the way your creature communicates?

7. Practice communicating the way creatures on your planet communicate.

Planet 4

The creatures from your planet may talk only with members of the opposite sex. If they want to say something to someone of the same sex, they must get someone from the opposite sex to relay their message. In the same way, they can listen only to someone of the opposite sex. If someone of the same sex tries to speak to them, they turn away, and ask someone of the opposite sex to relay the message.

Please work together as a group to answer the following questions:

1. What is the name of your planet?

2. What does your creature look like?
(Please draw a picture on a separate piece of paper)

3. What is the weather like on your planet?

4. What does your creature eat?

5. What is the best thing about the way your creature communicates?

6. What is the hardest thing about the way your creature communicates?

7. Practice communicating the way creatures on your planet communicate.

Planet 5

The creatures from your planet can talk only when they have direct eye contact with the other person. If the other person looks away, they must stop talking until they can look into the other person's eyes.

Please work together as a group to answer the following questions:

1. What is the name of your planet?

2. What does your creature look like?
(Please draw a picture on a separate piece of paper)

3. What is the weather like on your planet?

4. What does your creature eat?

5. What is the best thing about the way your creature communicates?

6. What is the hardest thing about the way your creature communicates?

7. Practice communicating the way creatures on your planet communicate.

16 BASIC NEEDS AROUND THE WORLD

GRADE LEVELS: K-4, (5-6)

OBJECTIVES: To introduce the concept of universal basic needs; to define basic needs: food, clothing, shelter, love, physical safety. **Note:** This activity is a variation on Activity 1-14: "Human Needs." This version focuses more on the global aspects of human needs.

SUBJECT AREAS: Social studies, art

MATERIALS: Pictures of people from different cultures that show them meeting basic needs, magazines with pictures of people of different cultures (*National Geographic* is a good source), at least five large sheets of paper (16 x 32 or larger), scissors, paste

INSTRUCTIONS

1. Ask: What are the things people need to survive? List responses on the board under the label "Needs." Explain the difference between needs and wants: needs are things we must have to survive; wants are things we might desire but don't need for our survival. If students suggest wants, ask them: Is that something you need to survive? List wants on the board under the label "Wants." On the "Needs" list there will be items related to the basic needs of food, clothing, shelter, safety, and love. When students suggest items such as money, sneakers, or hospitals, help them to clarify how those are related to basic needs.

2. Show pictures of people from different cultures meeting their basic needs. Discuss each picture. Ask: How are people meeting basic needs in this picture? How do you meet that need? Emphasize that we all share the same needs, even though we meet them in different ways.

3. Label each sheet of large paper with one of the basic needs. Have students find pictures in magazines of people meeting their basic needs. Then have them paste the pictures to the appropriate sheet of paper.

DISCUSSION QUESTIONS

- What are some of the different ways people meet their basic needs?
- What factors influence how different people meet their needs?
- How can differences between people create problems?
- People in other cultures may look different from us, but what are some ways they are like us?

17 WHAT'S IT LIKE TO . . . AROUND THE WORLD?

GRADE LEVELS: K-6

OBJECTIVES: To explore similarities and differences between various cultures in the way they meet needs and wants

SUBJECT AREAS: Social studies, language arts

MATERIALS: Appropriate artifacts

INSTRUCTIONS

1. This activity builds on Activity 2-16: "Basic Needs Around the World." Once students have a sense of how basic needs are met in other cultures and countries, extend that theme. You might say: We've seen how different cultures and countries have different ways of meeting basic needs. They also have different ways of supplying what people want.

2. Choose a theme and collect materials, such as utensils or books, related to that theme. You may also want to invite guest speakers. Some themes that I've used:

• Children's books around the world
• Toys around the world
• Television around the world
• Animated cartoons
• Comic books
• Newspapers
• School supplies

DISCUSSION QUESTIONS

Note: These will vary depending upon the topic you are exploring. Generally you will want to have children point out similarities and differences they see and encourage them to think about how cultures have influenced each other.

18 GOVERNMENTS AROUND THE GLOBE

GRADE LEVELS: (4), 5-6

OBJECTIVES: To explore how different countries and cultures govern themselves; to develop research skills

SUBJECT AREAS: Social studies, reading, language arts

MATERIALS: Encyclopedias, reference works

INSTRUCTIONS

1. Ask students to tell you everything they know about how the United States is governed. List their contributions on the board in one of three columns: What we know, What we think we know, What we need to find out. Help them to find the answers to the questions raised in the last two columns. Before proceeding with the rest of this activity, they should have a basic understanding of what the three branches of government are and what they do. It would be helpful, but is not necessary, for them to grasp how a bill becomes a law.

2. Choose a sample country, such as Japan. Explain to students how they would go about researching what the government of Japan is like. Depending upon their level of research skills, you may need to show them how to look up encyclopedia articles, how to locate books about Japan in the library, and how to use the table of contents and index of books.

3. Divide students into research teams. Assign (or let groups choose) a country and have them research the government of that country. The goal is to develop research skills and to gain a general understanding of how other cultures govern themselves. It is not necessary for students to understand or explain how the British government works, for example. But they should be able to state how Parliament is similar to and different from Congress and how the prime minister is similar to and different from our president.

DISCUSSION QUESTIONS

- Why do people have governments?
- How do people influence their governments?
- What are some of the variations of democracy in the world?
- What are nondemocratic governments like? What countries have nondemocratic governments?

GOING FURTHER

An interesting variation is for students to follow up the activity by exploring past governmental structures. My students have been particularly interested in the governments of ancient Egypt, Rome, and China, various Native American tribes, medieval Europe, and colonial America.

19 THE GLOBAL CANDY BAR

GRADE LEVELS: (K-2), 3-6

OBJECTIVES: To introduce the concept of interconnectedness; to explore ways one product is dependent upon international cooperation

SUBJECT AREAS: Social studies

MATERIALS: A chocolate bar with almonds (this activity was designed with Hershey bar), chart paper with candy bar ingredients listed, world map or globe

INSTRUCTIONS

1. Hold up a Hershey bar and ask the class where it came from. Answers will probably include: from the store, from the chocolate factory, from Hershey, Pennsylvania. Explain that by looking at the label, you can tell that the bar was manufactured (made) in Hershey, Pennsylvania, where the Hershey company is located.

2. Post the ingredients chart. Explain that you copied it from the label of the candy bar. Ask: Where do you think each of these ingredients came from? Explain, using the world map, the source of the ingredients:

• Chocolate/cocoa from Ghana
• Almonds from Brazil
• Sugar from Dominican Republic
• Milk from Pennsylvania dairy farms
• Corn syrup from Iowa corn fields
• Paper wrapper from paper made by Canadian lumber mills

Tell them that the Hershey bar itself is sold all over the world.

3. Introduce the term "interconnectedness," relating it to the word "connected." Explain that the people of the world are all dependent on each other. Many of the products we use every day have sources outside of the United States. World trade is what carries materials and products from one place to another all over the world. Similarly, the actions of a group of people in one part of the world affect people in other parts of the world. Discuss: If there was a drought and no almonds grew in Brazil, what effect would that have on the Hershey bar? If there was a strike at the Canadian paper factory?

4. Have older students research how different products are made and how other people of the world contribute to creating those products.

DISCUSSION QUESTIONS

- How is world trade a cooperative activity?
- How does world trade affect you here at home? Our community?
- What are some ways we are connected to other people in the world?
- What are some things all the people of the world have in common?
- In what ways are they different?
- We've talked a lot about community. In what ways is the world a community? In what ways is it not a community?

20 EARTH ADS:
Posters for a World Community

GRADE LEVELS: K-6

OBJECTIVES: To create posters that carry a message of world community; to reinforce the concepts of interconnectedness and peace

SUBJECT AREAS: Art, social studies

MATERIALS: Poster paper, crayons or markers, magazines with pictures of people from different countries and cultures (*National Geographic*, *World*, and travel magazines are good sources)

INSTRUCTIONS

1. Discuss how posters convey an idea or information in clear, visual ways. Ask students for examples of posters they have seen that do this. Point out that posters often have slogans that summarize the message.

2. Remind students of discussions the class has had about community and international connectedness (or for younger children, the world family). What kind of slogan would they put on a poster about the world community? Examples: We're All One Family, It's a Small World, We Are the World.

3. Have students create posters that illustrate their slogans. Have them share their posters with the class, then display them for the school.

4. A variation is to have students make bumper stickers. When completed, these can be covered with clear contact paper and attached to a bumper.

DISCUSSION QUESTIONS

- What would you like people to learn from your poster?
- How does your poster convey its message?

Chapter Three:
PEACE AND CONFLICT

INTRODUCTION

Conflict is a fact of life. Without conflict there is no growth, no progress. There is just stagnation. Some people define peace as the absence of conflict, and some incorporate conflict into their definitions. My own feeling is that peace results from responding constructively to conflict. Not from getting rid of it, or suppressing it, or ignoring it, or rushing in to compromise and smooth things over.

This definition of peace acknowledges that there will always be conflict and that there are many ways to handle it. If we are to teach children about peace, we must teach them some of the many options–beyond violence and inaction–available to them for handling conflicts. Children who don't learn that there are many ways to handle conflict are the ones most likely to be victimized by it.

The activities in this chapter are designed to introduce students to the basic principles of conflict resolution and to give them a way to think about conflict and a common vocabulary with which to talk about it. Through them, children can learn how conflict can be used constructively. These activities do not constitute a complete curriculum in interpersonal conflict resolution. Rather, they will help you begin working with your students on issues of conflict and conflict resolution that will make it relatively easy for them to draw connections with larger conflicts.

Once children have a solid understanding of how conflict works in their lives, they will be able to apply that understanding to community, national, and even international conflicts. This is not to say that a dispute between two nations is the same as a fight on the playground; obviously there are differences. But, they are analogous. Children–and adults–learn something about international conflict by comparing it to interpersonal conflict. In my experience, children often do this spontaneously. While no one is asking that children understand conflict at an adult level, the comparison to interpersonal conflict helps them comprehend more complex conflicts in a way that is empowering. They are far less likely to be frightened by world issues and current events than if they have no understanding of conflict.

The activities in this chapter deal with understanding and resolving conflict generally. Teaching about controversial issues or societal conflicts in the elementary classroom is discussed in Appendix A: Teaching Controversial Issues to Elementary Children.

Teaching Considerations

Acknowledge with children that solving conflict can be difficult. Sometimes creative "win-win" solutions don't appear. Sometimes we have to give the situation more time or make do with the best alternative until we think of something better.

• In discussions about conflict, children often raise the question of violence. In my experience, it is best to deal with the issue matter-of-factly. Acknowledge that violence is one way people deal with conflict. Then move on to more effective ways to handle conflict. If you have a class that seems stuck on violence as the only viable solution, you might want to try Activity 3-4: "What about Fighting?"

• As much as possible, model the kind of conflict resolution you want children to use. This doesn't mean that you should negotiate every conflict you have with a child. That is neither practical nor appropriate. What it does mean is that you let children know what is negotiable and what isn't. Children who never see adults dealing constructively with conflict are unlikely to do so themselves.

Connecting to Larger Issues

Take advantage of spontaneous moments for teaching. When children bring in current events, ask them about the elements of conflict that are present. For example: Who is involved in this conflict? What is his or her point of view on the problem? What caused this conflict to escalate? What might help it to de-escalate?

• Be positive. Learning about societal conflicts can be confusing and frightening to children (see Appendix A: "Teaching Controversial Issues to Elementary Children." A positive problem-solving approach can help them come to terms with larger conflicts. Use what they know about interpersonal conflict resolution to make larger conflicts feel more manageable.

WHAT'S SO BAD/GOOD ABOUT CONFLICT?

GRADE LEVELS: (K-2), 3-6

OBJECTIVES: To explore how conflict can be negative; to explore how conflict can be positive

SUBJECT AREAS: Social studies, thinking skills

MATERIALS: Chalkboard and chalk or newsprint and markers

INSTRUCTIONS

1. Write "conflict" on the board and ask the class for a definition. (If they need help with a definition, explain that a conflict is a disagreement between two or more people, and give a few examples.) Ask the class: What do you think of when you hear the word "conflict"?

2. Have the class brainstorm all the associations they have with the word "conflict." You may either list their contributions or create a web chart.

DISCUSSION QUESTIONS

- Which words are negative? Which are positive? Which are neutral?
- Why do you think there are more negative words about conflict than positive or neutral ones?
- Describe a conflict you've had. Would you say it was positive or negative?
- Can anyone describe a conflict that ended in a positive way (where everyone involved felt good at the end or things changed for the better as a result)?

2 MAYBE EVERYONE CAN WIN

GRADE LEVELS: (K-2), 3-6

OBJECTIVES: To introduce the concept of win-win conflict resolution

SUBJECT AREAS: Reading, social skills

MATERIALS: Handout 3-2: "Four Different Endings"

INSTRUCTIONS

1. Explain: Today we are going to work with finding many solutions to a problem. We'll be especially interested in solutions that will work for both people in a conflict. We will call those win-win because both people win.

2. As a whole group look at this problem: Carlos wants to play with the class gerbil during his free time. Danny wants to use the gerbil for his science report; he is studying how long the gerbil can spin the wheel in its cage. Have the class brainstorm all the possible solutions.

3. Next place them on a grid:

☺ ☺ **WIN-WIN**	☺ ☹ **WIN-LOSE**
Both Carlos and Danny get what they want.	Carlos gets what he wants but Danny doesn't.
☹ ☺ **LOSE-WIN**	☹ ☹ **LOSE-LOSE**
Carlos doesn't gets what he wants but Danny does get what he wants.	Carlos doesn't get what he wants and Danny doesn't get what he wants.

4. Repeat the activity in cooperative groups of three or four students. Explain: I'm going to describe a problem between two girls named Maria and Jeanie. You are going to come up with as many ways for them to solve the problem as you can, just as we did before, but this time put your solutions into categories. Give each group Handout 3-2: "Four Different Endings." Ask the groups to list at least five solutions to the problem, then place these solutions into the appropriate categories:

☺ ☺ **WIN-WIN**	☺ ☹ **WIN-LOSE**
Maria gets what she wants and Jeanie gets what she wants.	Maria gets what he wants but Jeanie doesn't get what she wants.
☹ ☺ **LOSE-WIN**	☹ ☹ **LOSE-LOSE**
Maria doesn't gets what she wants but Jeanie gets what she wants.	Maria doesn't get what she wants and Jeanie doesn't get what she wants.

5. Have each group establish roles for each member. This encourages cooperation. Use these roles: time keeper, recorder (the one who writes the group's ideas on the sheet), praiser (the one who gives encouragement and praise for the ideas people think of), and checker (the one who checks over the categories in which the group places each solution and probes for accuracy.)

6. Read the class the following situation.

Maria has finished her report on her favorite hobby and chooses to play with the new board game in the classroom. She's not sure of the rules, so she wants to play with someone who won't make fun of her.

Jeanie says she gets the board game now because she's doing her hobby report on it and it's due by the end of school. Last week Jeanie made fun of Maria when they played checkers.

7. Reconvene the whole class. The recorder from each group reports two of the group's solutions. Create one grid on the board to bring together the solutions from each group. Discuss what it means to have a win-win solution.

DISCUSSION QUESTIONS

• Have you ever been in a conflict that ended lose-lose? How did it feel?
• How about win-lose?
• Have you ever been in or seen a conflict that ended win-win?
• How did that happen?

GOING FURTHER

For older students, the win-win grid can be applied to larger conflicts as well. For example, Carol Reid, a teacher in Charlotte, North Carolina, sent the following chart, which she filled out with her class based on their knowledge of current events and history. When the chart was finished, they tested it by comparing current events and historical events to the chart.

Ⓖ GOVERNMENT THAT WANTS CONTROL

WIN-WIN	WIN-LOSE
Ⓟ Ⓖ	Ⓟ Ⓖ
Treaty	Petitions
Agreements	Candlelight vigils
Pacts	Demonstrations
Compromises	Processions
Free multi-party elections	Strikes
	Masses of people working together
	Rebellion
	Revolution– violent or peaceful
LOSE-WIN	**LOSE-LOSE**
Ⓟ Ⓖ	Ⓟ Ⓖ
Imprisonment	Civil war
Torture	Interference by / Assistance from other countries trying to take control
Exile	Economic collapse
Military rule	
Building barriers	
Economic limitations (P)	
Economic privileges (G)	
Massacre	
Secret police	

(left axis label) Ⓟ PEOPLE WHO WANT FREEDOM

This activity is adapted from Discovery Sessions by Sarah Pirtle. Franklin Mediation Services, 10 Osgood St., Greenfield, MA 01301, pp. 24-26.

Handout 3-2
FOUR DIFFERENT ENDINGS

Invent solutions to the conflict that fit in these four boxes:

WIN-WIN	WIN-LOSE
Both people get what they want.	Person 1 gets what he or she wants but person 2 doesn't.
LOSE-WIN	**LOSE-LOSE**
Person 1 doesn't get what he or she wants but person 2 does.	Neither person gets what he or she wants.

3 PRACTICING PROBLEM SOLVING

GRADE LEVELS: K-6

OBJECTIVES: To introduce problem-solving procedure; to provide structured practice in resolving conflict

SUBJECT AREAS: Thinking skills, social skills

MATERIALS: Reading 1: "Conflict stories (K-2)," Reading 2: "Conflict Stories (3-6)"

INSTRUCTIONS

1. Explain that when there is a conflict, there is a problem. When trying to resolve conflicts, it helps to have a way to think about the problem and to attempt to solve it.

2. Place the following steps on the board:

(1) Define the problem
(2) Brainstorm solutions
(3) Choose a solution and act on it

3. Go over each step with the class. Point out that before the problem solving begins, the people in the conflict have to agree to work it out. In order for problem solving to work, they have to agree to really try to work it out, and to not yell or call names. They want to DE-escalate the conflict, not escalate it.

Emphasize that in step two they want to come up with as many possible solutions as they can. In step three they want to choose a solution(s) that is win-win.

4. Practice the problem solving method with the class by reading the first conflict story aloud. With the class, go through the method, applying each step to the situation in the story. For example, look at "Leon Loses Control." The problem can be defined this way: Leon and Stevie are having an argument about doing a puzzle. Now the puzzle is wrecked.

Encourage students to define problems in a way that does not affix blame. Defining the problem is not solving it, so you want as neutral a definition as possible. This is difficult, particularly for young children, so you will need to assist them.

Possible solutions to this problem are:

• Start over
• Fix the puzzle together
• Find new puzzles to do separately
• Make rules for working on puzzles
• Find another activity
• Apologize to each other
• Tell the teacher

Now go through the possible solutions and place a check mark by those that seem to have the most win-win potential. Then go through the list again and discuss how each of the potential solutions might work out. Have the students tell you which one seems to them the most likely to be win-win.

5. Repeat with another conflict story.

DISCUSSION QUESTIONS

• How do you decide if a solution might work?
• What are the possible consequences of this particular solution?
• What things does the solution need in order to work? (materials, the cooperation of the other person, involvement of a third part, etc.)

GOING FURTHER

The song "There is Always Something You Can Do" reinforces the idea of looking for nonviolent alternatives. The message of this song can be a useful tool to get children to "hear each other out" when anger and hurt feelings prevail; then to try for an agreement that seems fair to both sides. Children might also play-act such a scene.

Song
THERE IS ALWAYS SOMETHING YOU CAN DO
Words and Music by Sarah Pirtle

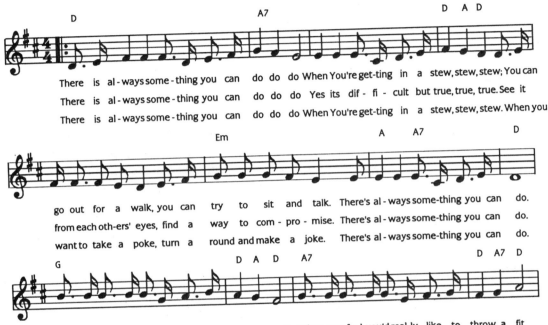

There is al-ways some-thing you can do do do When You're get-ting in a stew, stew, stew; You can
There is al-ways some-thing you can do do do Yes its dif-fi-cult but true, true, true. See it
There is al-ways some-thing you can do do do When You're get-ting in a stew, stew, stew. When you

go out for a walk, you can try to sit and talk. There's al-ways some-thing you can do.
from each oth-ers' eyes, find a way to com-pro-mise. There's al-ways some-thing you can do.
want to take a poke, turn a round and make a joke. There's al-ways some-thing you can do.

Wheth-er in a school or fam-'ly ar-gu-ment, When you feel you'd real-ly like to throw a fit
You can use your smarts and not your fist, fist, fist; You can give that probl-em a new twist, twist, twist

Don't be trapp'd by fights and fists and an-gry threats, Reach out for this or-din-ar-y plan. 2. There is
You can see it 'round a-bout and up-side down, Give your-self the time to find a way. 3. There is

Printed by permission of Sarah Pirtle. Recorded on Two Hands Hold the Earth by Sarah Pirtle. A Gentle Wind, Box 3103, Albany, NY 12203.

Reading
CONFLICT STORIES (K-2)

LEON LOSES CONTROL

Stevie and Leon were working on a puzzle together. Leon took a piece from Stevie and put it in place. Stevie got mad and wrecked the puzzle. Then he told the teacher that it was Leon's fault. "He's a tattletale and a fat liar!" Leon said.

BRENDA BATTLES BLANCA

Brenda and Blanca were drawing a mural together. Blanca slipped and her crayon made a big blue mark right across the people Brenda was drawing. "You wrecked the whole thing!" Brenda shouted. "You always wreck everything!"

Reading
CONFLICT STORIES (3-6)

SCIENCE PROJECT SQUABBLES

Paulo and Gina were supposed to be working on a science project. Every time they went to the library to work, Paulo wanted to look through books. Gina wanted them to outline their project. "I don't work the same way you do," said Paulo. "I get ideas when I look at books." "But we're never going to get anything done at the rate we're going," said Gina. "And I'm not going to do the whole thing."

MESSY MARTINEZ

One day Angel Martinez dropped his tray in the cafeteria. He slipped in the spaghetti and fell. He got tomato sauce, milk, and fruit cocktail all over him. From then on everyone called him "Messy Martinez." Angel hates to be called that, and he doesn't want to go to school anymore.

4 WHAT ABOUT FIGHTING?

GRADE LEVELS: (4), 5-6

OBJECTIVES: To identify the potential positive and negative consequences of using violence to resolve conflicts

SUBJECT AREAS: Social studies, language arts

MATERIALS: Chalkboard and chalk

INSTRUCTIONS

1. Ask students how they would define violence. Why do they think people sometimes use violence to handle conflicts?

2. After the students have offered a few suggestions, ask them to name everything positive they can think of about fighting or using violence to resolve conflicts. If they have trouble naming any, ask them to think about a fight they won. What feelings did they have? What positive things did the fight accomplish? List their contributions on the board. Continue the brainstorm for five to ten minutes until energy begins to lag.

3. Next ask students to name all the potential negative consequences of fighting or using violence to deal with conflicts. Repeat the brainstorming process. If necessary, ask about specific areas of students' lives: What might be the consequences of fighting at home? At school? On the playground? The negative list will probably be significantly longer.

DISCUSSION QUESTIONS

- Which list is longer? Why?
- Which of these negative things is a short term consequence? Which is long term?
- What are some ways you could get the positive effects of fighting without fighting?
- If there are so many reasons not to fight, why do people fight?
- Where do we get our ideas about fighting?

5 THE —ATE WORDS
(There Are Many Ways to Resolve Conflicts)

GRADE LEVELS: (K-2), 3-6

OBJECTIVES: To introduce the range of possible conflict resolution techniques; to introduce some of the technical terms of conflict resolution

SUBJECT AREAS: Language arts, social studies

MATERIALS: Handout 3-5: "The —Ate Words," conflict resolution skits (from Activity 3-8)

INSTRUCTIONS

1. Distribute Handout 3-5: "The —Ate Words." Explain that there are many ways people resolve conflicts, some of which have names. Read the handout with the class, discussing each of the terms. Ask students if they can think of examples of each kind of conflict resolution.

2. Read the following situations to the class and have students identify what type of conflict resolution is being used

Roger and Kindra were arguing over who would get to use the box of markers. They realized that arguing was getting them nowhere, so they figured out several ways they could both use the markers. Then they chose the way they liked best. **(NEGOTIATE)**

Jerome, Ted, and Alfredo are supposed to put up a bulletin board display together, but they can't agree on what the theme should be. They finally went to their teacher Mr. Nuñez and asked him to choose the bulletin board theme. **(ARBITRATE)**

Juanita was upset because her best friend Sara walked by her this morning without saying a word. She didn't speak to Sara all day. Finally Sara got Juanita to say what was wrong. "I didn't even see you," Sara cried. "I would never walk by without saying something to you." It was all a misunderstanding. **(COMMUNICATE)**

Ricardo and Diana were playing on the same softball team, but they both wanted to pitch. They were shouting at each other. Finally Monty came up and helped them work out a solution to the problem. **(MEDIATE)**

Marla was being teased and called names by some kids in the class. She hated being called names. Every morning the class had a class meeting to discuss things. Marla suggested that there be a class rule against name-calling and teasing. **(LEGISLATE)**

Carmen has accused Reba of stealing things out of her locker. They have taken their problem to the student court. The court is made up of a high school girl, who is the judge, and a jury of eighth- and ninth-graders. They will present evidence to the court. The jury will decide if Reba is guilty. If she is, the judge will decide her punishment. **(LITIGATE)**

3. Or have student volunteers read the conflict resolution skits from Activity 3-8. The audience can say what approach might be used to solve the conflict.

DISCUSSION QUESTIONS

- Have you used one of these conflict resolution approaches? Describe the situation.
- What are some other ways of resolving conflicts that are not on this handout? (compromise, problem solving, competing, using chance)

GOING FURTHER

Students will enjoy the poem "Ations" on page 59 of Shel Silverstein's *A Light In The Attic.*

Handout 3-5
THE —ATE WORDS

COMMUNICATE
Some conflicts start because people misunderstand each other. Talking things out and explaining might take care of it.

NEGOTIATE
When two or more people decide to work out a conflict themselves, they might follow a set of steps. The steps help them work out the conflict or *negotiate*.

MEDIATE
Sometimes people want to work out a problem but have trouble negotiating. They might ask someone to help them. That person is called a *mediator*. He or she *mediates* the conflict by helping the people work it out. The mediator does not tell the people what to do; he or she helps them decide for themselves.

ARBITRATE
Sometimes a mediator does solve people's problems. Then he or she isn't called a mediator. He or she is called an *arbitrator*. When people ask an arbitrator to help them, they must agree to do whatever the arbitrator says.

LITIGATE
When people can't work out their conflict themselves, they may go to a court and have a trial. They hire lawyers and go before a judge. A judge is like an arbitrator. The lawyers try to convince the judge that their client is right. The judge decides who is right according to the law and decides what solution there should be.

LEGISLATE
To legislate is to make something the law or a rule. Some kinds of conflicts cause people to try to change laws or rules so the problem won't happen again.

6 CONFLICT ESCALATES

GRADE LEVELS: (K-2), 3-6

OBJECTIVES: To introduce the concept of conflict escalating; to identify behaviors that cause conflict to escalate

SUBJECT AREAS: Language arts, thinking skills

MATERIALS: Conflict Escalator Stories, Handout 3-6: "The Conflict Escalator"

INSTRUCTIONS

1. Introduce the term "escalate," relating it to "escalator." Explain that when a conflict gets worse, people say it escalates.

2. Draw an escalator on the board as follows:

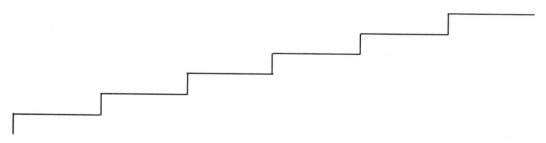

3. Read the first conflict escalator story aloud once. Then read it a second time and ask the class to signal you each time the conflict goes up another step on the escalator. Each time they identify an escalation step, write it on the escalator. Continue until you have reached the top of the escalator.

4. Review each step on the escalator and ask the class: What do you think the person was feeling at this step on the escalator? Write their responses under the escalator step. (There may be more than one feeling.)

5. Distribute Handout 3-6: "The Conflict Escalator." Read the second conflict escalator story, then repeat and have students write the steps of the escalation on their handouts. After they have completed the steps in the escalation, have them write the feelings they had underneath the escalation steps.

DISCUSSION QUESTIONS

- What happens to feelings as conflicts escalate?
- What makes conflicts escalate?
- When you are in a conflict, what puts you onto the escalator?
- How can you get on to the down escalator? (Or: How can you de-escalate conflicts?)

GOING FURTHER

Have students act out conflicts or use the conflict skit scripts. Then have them plot the escalation on the conflict escalator.

Reading
CONFLICT ESCALATOR STORIES

PENCIL PUSHING PROBLEMS

Jermaine and Janet sat at the same desk. Jermaine asked Janet if he could borrow a pencil. Janet was trying to hear the teacher so she said, "Will you shut up!"

This made Jermaine mad, so he pulled on Janet's braid.

Janet punched Jermaine in the arm.

Jermaine pushed her books on the floor.

The teacher said, "What's going on over there?"

Jermaine and Janet both pointed to each other and said, "He/she started it!"

A HAT FULL OF TROUBLE

Tyrone wanted a new ball cap, but couldn't get one. Shanda came to school wearing a new Red Sox cap and Tyrone told her it looked stupid.

Shanda said, "Not as stupid as that old one you wear."

Tyrone grabbed Shanda's cap and put it on his head. Shanda tried to grab it back, and it fell to the floor. Tyrone stepped on it to keep Shanda from picking it up and left a big footprint on the cap.

Shanda was furious. "You jerk! You're going to buy me a new cap!" she yelled. Then she grabbed Tyrone's shirt. When he tried to get away from her, his shirt ripped.

"You're going to buy me a new shirt," he yelled.

BROTHER BOTHERS BROTHER

Russell's younger brother Curtis borrowed Russell's bike without asking.

Russell was so angry he took Curtis's G. I. Joe Action figures and hid them.

Curtis got back by ripping a poster off Russell's wall.

Russell threw the action figures into the garbage.

Curtis took a rotten tomato out of the garbage and threw it in Curtis's face.

Now they are rolling on the kitchen floor fighting.

Handout 3-6
THE CONFLICT ESCALATOR

7 VERSUS VS. VERSUS
(Types of Conflict)

GRADE LEVELS: 3-6

OBJECTIVES: To introduce types of conflict

SUBJECT AREAS: Social studies, language arts

MATERIALS: Handout 3-7: "Versus vs. Versus"

INSTRUCTIONS

1. Explain to students that people divide conflicts into different types of categories. You might talk about "kid conflicts" and "adult conflicts," or "noisy conflicts" and "quiet conflicts." Ask: What are some types of conflicts that you can think of? List student suggestions on the board.

2. Distribute Handout 3-7: "Versus vs. Versus" and explain that it describes one way of categorizing conflicts. Explain that *versus* is a Latin word meaning "against" and that its abbreviation is "vs." Go over the handout and discuss each of the types of conflict.

DISCUSSION QUESTIONS

- Can you think of an example of each of these types of conflict?
- In what ways are all these types of conflict the same?
- In what ways are they different?
- What are some other ways you could categorize conflicts? (big or small, noisy or quiet, violent or nonviolent)

Handout 3-7
VERSUS VS. VERSUS

"Versus" means "against." The abbreviation or short form of "versus" is "vs."

We often use the word "versus" to show that people are in a conflict.

Why would a word that means "against" be used to show that people are in a conflict?

YOU VS. YOU

A conflict inside of you is called an "Internal Conflict."

PERSON VS. PERSON

A conflict between two or more people is called an "Interpersonal Conflict."

GROUP VS. GROUP

A conflict between groups of people is called an "Intergroup Conflict."

NATION VS. NATION

A conflict between countries is called an "International Conflict."

8 CONFLICT SKITS

GRADE LEVELS: 2-6

OBJECTIVES: To provide structured practice in resolving conflicts; to review the problem-solving technique for resolving conflicts

SUBJECT AREAS: Drama, reading, social skills, thinking skills

MATERIALS: Conflict-resolution skits, puppets for younger students

INSTRUCTIONS

1. After students have been introduced to the problem-solving approach to conflict resolution, give them a chance to practice using the conflict resolution skits.

2. Have student volunteers act out one of the skits. When they have finished, take the class through the problem solving approach. When the class has decided which solution it likes best, have the players act it out. Is it a win-win resolution? There may be several solutions the class likes. The actors may try acting out all of them.

3. Once older students have the idea of conflict resolution skits, have them work in small groups to create their own. They can present these to the class. They may even want to present them to younger children.

DISCUSSION QUESTIONS

- What makes the conflicts in the skits escalate?
- What words can people say to indicate that they want to stop the fight and try to solve the problem?
- Have you ever had a conflict like this one? How did you resolve it?

Script
THE TAPE RECORDER FIGHT

Characters:

Student 1: Wants to use the tape recorder
Student 2: Is using the tape recorder

Scene: A classroom

1: Quick! I've got to use the tape recorder!

2: But I'm using it now. I'm listening to this story.

1: That's not important. We need it for this play we're doing.

2: Can I be in the play?

1: No—we already have enough people. There's no room for you.

2: (pauses) I'm using the tape recorder.

1: Don't be a jerk! You can listen to that story anytime.
We really need it now!

2: So do I.

1: No you don't. See if I do anything for you ever again.
You slob! You pig! You jerk!

2: Oh! I'm telling on you!

1: I'm telling on you too, creep face!

Script
THE TV FIGHT

Characters:

Student 1: The older brother or sister wo is watching TV
Student 2: The younger brother or sister

(**1** is watching TV. **2** comes in and changes the channel.)

1: Hey! I was watching that!

2: I want to watch "Masters of the Universe."

1: Too bad. I was here first. (Changes the channel back.)

2: You always get to watch what you want. (Changes channel.)

1: Mom!

2: Mom's not here and I don't have anything to do because you won't play with me.

1: (Changes channel back.) So watch this with me.

2: No! You're supposed to take care of me when Mom's not here and you're not. So let me watch what I want to watch or I'll tell.

1: You're such a baby, you think you can always get what you want.

2: You think you can do what you want because you're bigger. (Starts to change channel again.)

1: You change that channel and I'll get you.

2: I'm going to wreck your room! (Runs out.)

1: You touch anything in my room and you're in trouble! (Runs after.)

9 PICTURE THE CONFLICT

GRADE LEVELS: K-6

OBJECTIVES: To discuss how conflict is a natural part of life; to explore how conflict takes place at many levels

SUBJECT AREAS: Language arts, social studies

MATERIALS: Pictures cut from magazines and mounted on construction paper. Choose a range of pictures. A representative sample could include everyday objects such as a watch, a pack of cigarettes, sneakers, a TV, and a VCR. Try to find pictures that will extend the concept to other levels, such as a community meeting, a soldier or a war, professional athletics events, a police car. Finally, try to find pictures of the president and of a well-known social activist like Martin Luther King, Jr.

INSTRUCTIONS

Show the pictures one at a time and discuss as suggested below. Accept all student responses, asking them to clarify when necessary and emphasizing that conflict takes many forms and takes place at many levels. (For example: A picture of a pack of cigarettes could represent conflict between kids and parents, between smokers and nonsmokers, between an official and someone smoking where it is not allowed, between legislators and various lobbying groups.)

DISCUSSION QUESTIONS

- What do you see in this picture? What could this have to do with conflict?
- Are there other conflicts that could be related to this picture?
- Have you ever had a conflict over something like this?

10 POINT OF VIEW

GRADE LEVELS: K-3

OBJECTIVES: To explore the role of perspective in conflicts; to practice looking at different perspectives

SUBJECT AREAS: Reading, language arts, thinking skills

MATERIALS: Magazine picture of a box of cookies; *The Owl and the Woodpecker* by Brian Wildsmith (Franklin Watts, 1971); Handout 3-10: "Animal Opinions"

Summary

The Woodpecker sleeps all night and works all day, while the Owl, who lives nearby, works all night and sleeps all day–or would sleep all day if the Woodpecker didn't keep him awake. The other animals in the forest take sides in the dispute, but finally they agree that a solution must be found to the problem.

INSTRUCTIONS

1. Introduce the concept of perspective by introducing the term point of view. Explain that someone's point of view is the way he or she looks at something. Different people can have different points of view on the same thing.

2. Hold up the picture of the cookies. Ask: What is your point of view on these cookies? Most students will respond positively. If any do not, ask them to explain why. It will probably be that they don't like that particular brand or type of cookie. Note that what seems delicious to one person is not so to another.

3. Ask: If you had just finished a box of these cookies by yourself, what would your point of view be? If you were sick in bed, what would your point of view be? Note that different circumstances can affect our points of view.

4. Explain that our point of view is based in part on our experiences in the past. For example:

Two kindergarten children walk past someone's yard. The yard is surrounded by a chain link fence. There is a dog jumping against the fence and barking at the children as they walk by. The first child says, "Oh look at that big, friendly dog. It's saying 'hi!' to us." The second child says, "Let's get out of here. That dog is trying to jump the fence and bite us!"

Discuss why two children might have such different reactions to the same situation. How might their points of view affect their behavior? How might they lead to conflict between them?

5. Read *The Owl and the Woodpecker* by Brian Wildsmith. Prior to reading the story, ask students to pay particular attention to the various points of view. When you have finished reading, ask for two volunteers, one to be the Owl, the other to be the Woodpecker. Have each child explain the point of view of his or her character and why the character has that point of view. Discuss how differing points of view led to conflict.

6. Second and third-graders can complete Handout 3-10: "Animal Opinions." You may want to have them do the handout in pairs or groups of three. When everyone has completed the handout, review the answers. For younger students use the handout as a discussion guide.

DISCUSSION QUESTIONS

- How does our point of view affect how we behave?
- What are some conflicts you've had or seen that were caused by different points of view?
- How could a better understanding of the other person's point of view help you resolve a conflict?

ANIMAL OPINIONS

The animals in the book *The Owl and the Woodpecker* all had different opinions on the conflict between the Owl and the Woodpecker. Read the statements below and write the name of the animal who probably expressed that opinion. (You will use some of the animals twice.)

Animal names:	Badger	Mouse
	Bear	Owl
	Beaver	Woodpecker
	Fox	

"This tree looks delicious!"

_____

"That Owl always chases us. He should be the one to move away."

_____

"The Woodpecker was here first. It's only fair that the Owl move."

_____

"This is my tree. So what if I make noise. If you don't like it, move!"

_____

"I like it here and I'm not going to move. You should keep quiet."

"We like it quiet here in the forest. Keep still!"

"We will have to make the Owl move. Let's push down his tree."

"Oh no! The storm is going to blow Owl's tree down. I must wake him."

"He saved my life. I'll be his friend forever."

UNDERSTANDING ANOTHER'S PERSPECTIVE

GRADE LEVELS: 3-6

OBJECTIVES: To provide further practice in looking at situations from varying points of view

SUBJECT AREAS: Reading, language arts, art

MATERIALS: Children's books with conflict themes, art materials

INSTRUCTIONS

1. Have students rewrite fairy tales from the point of view of the villain. For example, they can retell "Jack and the Beanstalk" from the point of view of the giant. They might also try retelling the story from the point of view of several characters, as if they were telling each character's side in a court of law.

2. Have students take a scene from a book they have read and tell it from the points of view of three different characters in the book, explaining how each would see it. They can then illustrate their descriptions.

3. Have students choose a character from a book they have read and write a letter to that character. Then they should write a response to the letter that is like what they think the character would say. They should continue the correspondence until there are at least four letters.

4. Ask students to draw a picture of a conflict situation. Then have them write a description of the situation from the point of view of a neutral observer. Next, have them draw how the conflict would look to a bird in the air (or a fly on the ceiling), then how it would look to an ant on the ground or underneath the conflict looking up. Continue with as many points of view as you wish, such as that of the furniture in the room, other people or animals who might be watching, etc. If you wish, you can have students write short descriptions of each point of view after they draw.

DISCUSSION QUESTIONS

- What do you learn about people or situations when you look at them from different points of view?
- How might that help you understand conflicts?

12 POSITIONS AND INTERESTS

GRADE LEVELS: 4-6

OBJECTIVES: To introduce the terms "positions" and "interests"; to practice identifying positions and interests

SUBJECT AREAS: Language arts, social studies

MATERIALS: Handout 3-12: "Positions and Interests in Negotiating"

INSTRUCTIONS

1. Introduce Positions and Interests. Explain that people in conflicts often have something they want. That is their position. There are reasons why they want what they want. These reasons are called their interests. It is easier to find win-win resolutions to conflicts when you look at interests, not just positions.

For example:

> Two kindergarten children are arguing over a truck. They are both saying "I want it! " The position of each child is that he or she should have the truck. The first child wants to "drive" the truck through a tunnel he made out of blocks. That is his interest. The second child wants to give her stuffed animal a ride on the truck. That is her interest.

2. Distribute Handout 3-12: "Positions and Interests in Negotiating." Read the first half aloud with students. Discuss the questions raised. Emphasize that if the mother had asked what the girls' interests were, she could have helped them find a solution that would meet their interests.

3. Have students complete the "You Try It" section of the worksheet. Then have them share and discuss responses.

DISCUSSION QUESTIONS

- Now that we've identified some of Sam's and Roger's interests, can you think of a solution to their conflict that would meet both their interests?
- How could you find out what someone's interests are?
- Can you think of a conflict you've had where you were "stuck" because you only looked at positions, not interests?

GOING FURTHER

Have students bring in accounts of conflicts from the newspaper. These may be any type of conflict from interpersonal to international. Have the class identify the positions and interests in the conflict.

Handout 3-12
POSITIONS AND INTERESTS IN NEGOTIATING

When people have a conflict, they often have a POSITION. Their position is what they say they want. They also have INTERESTS. Interests are the reasons they want what they want. Read this story:

Two little girls were arguing over an orange. "I want it!" shouted the first girl. "I want it!" shouted the second girl. Their mother came in and listened to each girl's position. Then she took a knife and cut the orange in half. She gave each girl a half.

The first girl peeled her half of the orange, threw away the peel and ate the inside. The second girl peeled her half of the orange, threw away the inside and grated up the peel. She was making orange cookies.

· What was each girl's position?

· What was the first girl's interest? What was the second girl's interest?

· If the mother had listened to their interests, how might the resolution of the conflict been different?

You Try It

Read the following situation and decide what you think the interests might be.

Roger and Sam are friends and are discussing what to do together on a Saturday afternoon. Roger wants to go shopping to get a new fall jacket for school. Sam wants to go to the beach and lie in the sun–there won't be many nice days left.

What is Roger's position? _____

What is Sam's position? _____

What might be some of Roger's interests? _____

_____

_____

What might be some of Sam's interests? _____

_____

_____

Remember: Looking only at positions is one way people get "stuck" when they try to resolve conflicts. Look at interests, not positions.

13 TOM AND MOM: Win-Win Negotiating

GRADE LEVELS: 4-6

OBJECTIVES: To introduce the process of win-win negotiation; to give students an opportunity to practice win-win negotiation by role-playing

SUBJECT AREAS: Language arts, social studies, drama

MATERIALS: Tom and Mom role-play cards; Handout 3-13: "The Win-Win Negotiation Process"; markers and large sheets of paper

INSTRUCTIONS

Note: Do Activity 3-12: "Positions and Interests" before doing this activity.

1. Introduce the term "negotiation" (or review the meaning if you did Activity 3-5: "The -Ate Words" with your class). Negotiation is two or more people working out an agreement, usually by following a series of steps. "Win-win negotiating" is trying to come to an agreement that meets the needs or interests of all the people involved. Ask students for examples of negotiation. (Some possibilities: when adults buy houses, when nations develop peace treaties.)

2. Distribute Handout 3-13: "The Win-Win Negotiation Process." Have the class read the handout, looking for similarities and differences between win-win negotiation and problem-solving. They will probably point out step one, "Identify Positions and Interests." If necessary, review that *positions* are what people say they want in a conflict. *Interests* are the reasons they want what they want.

3. Divide the class in half. One group will play the role of Tom. The other will play the role of Mom. Give all the Toms a copy of the role-play card "Tom." Give all the Moms a copy of the "Mom" role-play card. Have the Moms and the Toms meet in separate groups and determine what their positions and interests are. There should be one position. There may be many interests. When the groups are finished, record the positions and interests on large sheets of paper.

4. Have one Mom and one Tom role play presenting and listening to each other's positions and interests. Stress the need for each to be specific when presenting his or her point of view, and to avoid name-calling. The rest of the class should be observers. They should listen for communication between Tom and Mom that is helpful and not helpful. Discuss what they observed when Mom and Tom have finished. (If you need to do this lesson in two sessions, this is good place to stop.)

5. Have the Moms and Toms regroup and brainstorm possible solutions to the problem. Encourage them to come up with as many solutions as possible without judging them. (That will happen in the next step.) Bring the whole class back together to share their lists. Record the possible solutions on the board.

6. With the whole class, eliminate those solutions that are unacceptable to either part. Both parties have the right to strike out any solutions that do not, for whatever reason, meet their needs.

7. Have the class select a solution that best meets the needs of both parties. Encourage students to state why it meets the interests of both Mom and Tom.

8. Have the class make a plan to take action. The group should specify how the plan will be implemented.

DISCUSSION QUESTIONS

- How is the win-win negotiation process similar to the problem-solving technique we used? How is it different?
- When Mom and Tom presented their positions and interests to each other, what helped them communicate? What blocked communication?
- What might be a situation where you could use the win-win negotiation process?
- What conditions do you think are necessary for good negotiations?

GOING FURTHER

Have students think of historical conflicts they might negotiate. Some examples are: Columbus negotiating with Ferdinand and Isabella, King John and the nobles negotiating the Magna Carta, the Constitutional Convention, etc. Have them develop role-plays based on historical conflicts.

The "Win-Win Negotiation Process" was adapted from Roger Fisher and William Ury, Getting to Yes. Houghton Mifflin, *Boston, 1981.*

Handout 3-13
THE WIN-WIN NEGOTIATION PROCESS

1. Identify Positions and Interests

When you negotiate, "positions" are what you say you want. "Interests" are the reasons you want it.

2. Present and Listen

You should say what your positions and interests are. You then listen when the person you're negotiating with says what his or her positions and interests are. Try not to call names. Try to be specific.

3. Brainstorm Possible Solutions

Think of all the ways to solve the problem that you can. Try to think of lots. Write them down. Don't say if the ideas are good or bad. That will happen next.

4. Eliminate Solutions That Are Unacceptable

Read over all the ideas. Draw a line through any ideas that either of you doesn't like.

5. Choose a Solution That Will Meet the Interests of Everybody

Read the ideas that are left on your list. Choose the idea or ideas that will meet everyone's interests. You want to help everyone feel like a winner.

6. Make a Plan to Take Action

Once you choose a solution, decide how you will make sure it happens. Decide what the first steps will be. Decide who will do what and when they will do it.

Role-Play Cards
TOM AND MOM

TOM: You are a boy, 11 years old.

Your allowance is $1 a week. You want $3 a week. Many of your friends get $3. You do a lot of work around the house and think that you deserve to get $3 a week. Also, you want to save money to buy Nintendo Games because you and your friends like to play them together. At $1 a week, it will take forever; so why bother? With $3 a week, you will really be able to save money.

MOM: You are a single mother.

It would be hard, but not impossible, for you to afford $3 a week. You feel that Tom is not always reliable about doing his chores around the house. You don't think he should be rewarded with a bigger allowance if he's not going to be responsible. Also, Tom always says he will save money for things, but he doesn't. He just wastes money.

14 THE PETER RABBIT MEDIATION

GRADE LEVELS: 2-5

OBJECTIVES: To introduce principles of mediation; to practice mediation

SUBJECT AREAS: Reading, language arts, social skills, thinking skills

MATERIALS: Role-play cards, Handout 3-14: "The ABCs of Mediation"

INSTRUCTIONS

1. Remind students that mediation is a way of helping people resolve their conflicts. Sometimes people get so angry, or their conflict is so difficult, they can't resolve it by themselves and they need help. They might agree to ask a mediator for help.

2. The mediator helps the people who have a conflict use the problem-solving approach learned in Activity 3-3: "Practicing Problem Solving." Distribute Handout 3-14: "The ABCs of Mediation" and review the steps with the class. The mediator is trying to determine:

• What's the problem?
• What can we do about it?
• What's the best thing we can do?

The mediator also sets up certain ground rules:

• One person talks at a time
• Everyone tells the truth
• No name-calling or put downs

3. Model the process with two student volunteers. Use the tape recorder fight in Activity 3-8 as a sample, with yourself as the mediator.

4. Explain that the class will practice mediation by solving a conflict in a book they may have read or heard when they were younger. Ask for volunteers to review, briefly, the plot from *The Tale of Peter Rabbit.* Explain that they will be working in groups of four to resolve the conflict between Mr. MacGregor and Peter Rabbit. One person in the group will be Peter, one will be Mr. MacGregor, one will be the mediator, and one will be an observer.

5. Assign students to groups of four and assign them their roles. Give the appropriate role-play cards to students. Allow fifteen to twenty minutes for them to come up with a win-win resolution. You may want to help the process by saying after five minutes, "Time to start choosing a win-win resolution," and after ten minutes or so, "Time to start choosing a win-win resolution."

6. Stop the process after twenty minutes, whether or not all the groups are finished. Have the observer from each group report on the resolution that was reached.

DISCUSSION QUESTIONS

- What was it like to have someone help you come to a resolution?
- How did it help? How did it make things more difficult?
- What did you observers notice about _____ ?
- How might mediation contribute to a more peaceful world?

GOING FURTHER

You can repeat this process with the other folk or fairy tales such as *Goldilocks and the Three Bears, Peter and the Wolf,* and *Jack and the Beanstalk.*

Role-Play Cards
PETER RABBIT

PETER RABBIT

I feel _____ . I feel this way because Mr. MacGregor says I tore up his garden. I went into the garden to play. I took only a few bites of some things. They looked so good.

Mr. MacGregor shouldn't have chased me with his hoe. I was very scared. He shouldn't have taken my shoes and my jacket. My mother will be mad. We can't afford new ones.

MR. MACGREGOR

I feel _____ . I feel this way because that rabbit was in my garden. He ate everything in sight. He made a mess.

I work very hard on my garden. My family needs the food I grow. Peter destroys property. This time he wrecked a fence and the potting shed too. I used his coat and shoes for a scarecrow. He owes me that.

MEDIATOR

Mr. MacGregor is accusing Peter Rabbit of stealing from his garden and ruining it. Peter says that he was in the garden. He says that he didn't hurt anything. He says Mr. MacGregor has stolen his coat and shoes.

You need to help them come to an agreement. Follow the directions on the sheet "The ABCs of Mediation."

Handout 3-14
THE ABCs OF MEDIATION

Introduce yourself. Ask if they want help solving the problem.

Review the ground rules:

• One person talks at a time.
• No name-calling or put-downs.
• Be honest.

(A) Ask Questions

• Decide who will speak first.
• Ask each person: What happened? How did it make you feel?
• After each person talks, summarize what was said.
• Say what you think the problem is.

(B) Brainstorm Possible Solutions

• Get ideas from each person about how to solve each part of the problem.
• Don't let them criticize the ideas right now. That happens next.
• If there are a lot of ideas, write them down.

(C) Choose Solutions

• Good solutions make everyone feel like a winner.
• Be specific. The solution should say Who, What, When, Where, How, How Much.
• Check to see if the solution is realistic and fair.
• Write it down and read it back to them.

Adapted from Fussbusters by Paul Godfrey and Barbara Davis, The Mediation Center, Asheville, N.C., 1986.

15 FROM THE PLAYGROUND TO THE WORLD

GRADE LEVELS: 3-6

OBJECTIVES: To observe and classify conflicts; to make connections between the interpersonal to the international

SUBJECT AREAS: Writing

MATERIALS: Pencil and paper or newsprint, 3 x 5 cards

INSTRUCTIONS

1. For a few days have students observe conflicts at recess time. Ask them to record the conflicts on 3 x 5 cards.

2. After students have several cards with conflicts, have them meet in small groups to share their observations and classify the types of conflicts they observed. They might classify them on the basis of who was involved, the type of behavior, the way the conflict escalated, etc. Some examples are: name-calling conflicts, yelling matches, conflicts about who owns something, etc.

3. Have group spokespeople share the categories their groups have developed. List these on a sheet of newsprint. Once several are listed, ask students if they know of any community, national, or international conflicts that fit these categories. Discuss any examples students suggest. Ask students to look for examples of these conflict categories in the newspaper and television news.

DISCUSSION QUESTIONS

- What kinds of conflicts do adults have?
- What are some of the ways adults resolve conflicts?
- After thinking about international conflicts, are there new categories you might add to our list?

This activity is based on an idea from Ellen Davidson.

16 CONTROVERSIAL ISSUES— CONFLICTS IN SOCIETY

GRADE LEVELS: 3-6

OBJECTIVES: To make the connection between interpersonal conflict and conflict at other levels

SUBJECT AREAS: Social studies, thinking skills

MATERIALS: Newspapers

INSTRUCTIONS

1. Ask: What kinds of conflicts do grown-ups have? List these on the board, categorizing them as "internal," "interpersonal," "intergroup," etc. Remind the students of these terms from Handout 3-7: "Versus vs. Versus." Try to elicit some examples of each type of conflict. Most, if not all, of their contributions will be very active, concrete types of conflict: arguments, robberies, etc.

2. Explain: There can be conflicts that we call "controversial issues." Controversial issues are problems in the community, the country, or the world. The conflicts that result are usually over how to solve these problems. Different people have different ideas about how the problems should be fixed.

3. Help the class develop a new list of controversial issues or societal conflicts. Older students can look through the newspaper and cut out stories about controversial issues.

DISCUSSION QUESTIONS

Note: In discussing controversial issues, you should choose a specific example to use in framing questions. Change the example with each question.

- Controversial issues can exist on many levels at the same time. How could a controversial issue like hunger be internal, interpersonal, intergroup, etc.?
- Where do people get information about controversial issues?
- What kind of decisions do people need to make about controversial issues?
- What are some of the ways adults resolve conflicts over controversial issues?

Chapter Four:
PEACE AND DIVERSITY

INTRODUCTION

One of my students once told me, with the candor of a second-grader, why she appreciated the diversity in our classroom. "Michael's my friend," she said, "because he raises rabbits and I raise gerbils. Reba's my friend because we share snacks and I like the way black skin looks with white skin. Melania's my friend because we sit next to each other and I like her accent. Ellie's my friend because she has five Barbies and lets me play with any one I want." This girl understood in very concrete terms how diversity enriched her life.

Diversity can be enriching for both people and societies. It broadens our outlook and exposes us to new ideas and new ways of doing things. One aspect of a peaceable community is recognizing and celebrating difference.

But it would be naive to pretend that there are not problems associated with diversity. With diversity comes conflict, and while that is not inherently bad, it does present challenges. Just as children need to learn the skills of responding creatively to conflict, so they need to learn the skills of appreciating and dealing with diversity.

This chapter has two parts. The activities in the first part (numbers 1-4) are designed to help students recognize and celebrate the positive aspects of diversity. The activities in the second part (numbers 5-13) focus on helping students acquire the concepts and understanding they need in order to deal with the more challenging side of diversity: stereotyping, prejudice, and discrimination.

These activities deal with diversity and difference in a general way in the context of the classroom community. They are not sufficient for nor intended as a program for reducing prejudice. Neither do they deal, except peripherally, with such issues as equity or cultural pluralism. For more in-depth work on these issues, see the resources section below.

Teaching Considerations

Refer often to the values of diversity. I've found that it is helpful to have catch phrases that highlight an acceptance of diversity or point up its value: "She's marching to her own drummer," "He's got his own style," "Different strokes for different folks," "There are different roads to the same destination."

• When doing the activities in this chapter, students might express prejudiced attitudes or make racist remarks. You can be respectful of students as you set standards and explain why a remark might be objectionable. Some ways that teachers have addressed this problem are:

- Remind students about class standards: That's a put-down. We agreed that we don't use put-downs in this room.
- Reframe the remark and give students an alternative: The word we use in this room is gay man. We do not say "faggot."
- Encourage the student to think about what is behind the remark: There seem to be a lot of jokes about Japanese people lately. Why do you think that is?
- Ignore it. Sometimes it's simply a thoughtless joke or isolated incident.
- Be mindful of the student's feelings. Embarrassing the student who makes a racist comment is not likely to encourage that student to change or rethink his or her attitudes.
- Whenever possible, arrange for students to have positive interactions with people about whom they might have prejudices.

Connecting to Larger Issues

One very effective way to help students see connections between diversity at the personal level and at other levels is to use literature. Madeline L'Engle's *A Wrinkle in Time* celebrates difference by showing what a world without diversity might be like. Emily Cheney Neville's *Berries Goodman* shows how prejudice (in this case anti-semitism) affects two ordinary American children. Mildred Taylor's *Roll of Thunder Hear My Cry* vividly shows how black Americans have dealt with the personal effects of racism. Check the bibliography of children's trade books at the end of this chapter.

• As older children learn the language and concepts of diversity, particularly stereotyping, prejudice, and discrimination, have them look for examples in the news at the local, national, and international levels.

LOOK AT US!

GRADE LEVELS: 2-6

OBJECTIVES: To identify common interests, likes, and dislikes among community members

SUBJECT AREAS: Social skills, social studies, language arts

MATERIALS: Handout 4-1: "Commonalities"

INSTRUCTIONS

1. Begin by discussing some of the things that all the class members have in common. List these on the board. Then list some differences.

2. Distribute Handout 4-1: "Commonalities." Ask the students to fill in their preferences and experiences. Then, when you signal, they may mill about in a quiet and orderly manner, and should find people who share those preferences and experiences. Explain: "For each entry, find a different person who has something in common with you. You may not use the same person more than once."

DISCUSSION QUESTIONS

- Were there any surprises? Did you find that you had things in common with people you didn't think you would?
- How did it feel to look for commonalities?
- What might commonalities have to do with building a caring community? With peace?

This is a variation of an activity from Ellen Davidson.

Handout 4-1
COMMONALITIES

One of Your: **Someone who feels the same:**

Favorite kinds of cookies

_____   _____

Hobbies

_____   _____

Pet Peeves

_____   _____

Best subjects

_____   _____

Favorite ways to relax

_____   _____

Most recent trips

_____   _____

Favorite animals

_____   _____

Least favorite animals

_____   _____

Best birthday gifts

_____   _____

Favorite movies

_____   _____

2 SOMEDAY I'M GOING TO . . .

GRADE LEVELS: K-6

OBJECTIVES: To discover the range of aspirations and talents in the class; to help students get acquainted with each other

SUBJECT AREAS: Language arts, social studies

MATERIALS: Deck of playing cards, arranged in order: aces, twos, threes, etc.

INSTRUCTIONS

1. Introduce the game by asking students to imagine all the different jobs or occupations they might like to have someday. Encourage them to think of as many as they can by focusing on things they are good at and things they dream about doing.

2. Give each child a playing card. Deal the cards from the top of the deck. Explain that these are their business cards. People often exchange business cards when they first meet. They will be exchanging cards in this activity.

3. Explain that when you give the signal, students should go up to someone, exchange cards, and say what they do for a living (based on what they would like to do). It helps if you demonstrate first. They will have five minutes in which to meet as many people as possible. For each person they should try to think of something different.

4. With older children: After five minutes have them find a partner who has a card with the same number and the same color as on their own playing card (two of spades with two of clubs). Each person gets five minutes to talk about the different jobs he or she mentioned in the first part of the activity. They should say what jobs they mentioned and why.

5. Finish by having the pairs combine into groups of four; all the aces, all the twos, etc. Each person introduces his or her partner and explains what was learned about them in their interview.

DISCUSSION QUESTIONS

• How did it feel to imagine yourself in these different occupations?
• Did you have any difficulty imagining yourself in a lot of different jobs?
• Which of your fantasy jobs did you like best? Why?
• Were you surprised by anything you learned about people in this room?

Adapted from What is Cooperative Learning? Tips for Teachers and Trainers *by Nancy and Ted Graves. Cooperative College of California, 136 Liberty St., Santa Cruz, CA 95060, p. 342.*

3 TALENT SEARCH

GRADE LEVELS: 3-6

OBJECTIVES: To help students get acquainted; to encourage students to honor and value the unique attributes of their classmates

SUBJECT AREAS: Language arts

MATERIALS: Handout 4-3: "Talent Search"

INSTRUCTIONS

1. You may choose to use this activity to follow up on "Commonalities." Give each student a copy of Handout 4-3: "Talent Search."

2. Students should look for someone who fits each description. When they find someone who does, that person should sign the handout in the appropriate space. No one person can sign more than two entries on the handout.

DISCUSSION QUESTIONS

- Who did you discover in the class who . . . ? (List name on the board)
- Is there anyone else in the class who . . . ? (Add these names to the list)
- Were you surprised to find out some of the talents and experiences of your classmates?
- How can these talents and experiences enrich our community?
- How can these talents and experiences contribute to peace in our community?

Handout 4-3
TALENT SEARCH

Find someone who can say something in another language.

Find someone who plays a musical instrument. What is it?

Find someone who plays a team sport. What is it?

Find someone who likes to read science fiction books. What's a favorite?

Find someone who knows how to bake cookies. What kind?

Find someone who has ridden on a horse. Where was it?

Find someone who was born in another country. What country?

Find someone who has gone to this school since kindergarten.

Find someone who sings in a choir. Where is the choir?

Find someone who likes to build things. What have they made recently?

4 RAINBOW BOARD

GRADE LEVELS: K-2, (3-6)

OBJECTIVES: To affirm the various ways children contribute to the classroom community; to create a rainbow bulletin board

SUBJECT AREAS: Art, social skills

MATERIALS: Construction paper in the following colors, cut into 4" x 8" strips: red, blue, green, yellow, orange, purple. There should be enough strips for each child to have three.

INSTRUCTIONS

1. Begin by reviewing the behaviors that contribute to a caring classroom community. Ask students: What is something you have done that has contributed to building a caring community in our classroom? How have you helped our classroom be a place of peace?

2. Give each child three strips of paper, each of a different color. On each strip the children should write their name and something they do that contributes to a caring community. Examples are: "I don't hit people," "I help people who need help," "I put the puppets away."

3. Mount the strips on the bulletin board arranged in rainbow fashion. Point out that there are many talents in the room and many ways people contribute to a caring community. Add that everyone has something to contribute to the community, and when all of those different contributions are put together, it is like a rainbow.

4. Older students can set "caring goals." For each caring activity they write, they can also write a caring goal. For example, "I don't call people names" might be followed by "I will try to argue less during games." Encourage goals that are specific and measurable.

DISCUSSION QUESTIONS

- When you look at the rainbow, do you get any new ideas about how you could contribute to our classroom community?
- Even though we have many people contributing to our community, we still have problems we need to solve. What are some of those problems? How could we solve them?

5 ALL THE ANIMALS WERE ANGRY

GRADE LEVELS: K-4

OBJECTIVES: To identify problems associated with diversity; to discuss how to solve those problems.

SUBJECT AREAS: Reading, language arts

MATERIALS: *All the Animals Were Angry* by William Wondriska (Holt, Rhinehart and Winston, 1970); Handout 4-5: "It Helps and It Doesn't"

Summary

On a hot, boring day in the jungle, all the animals begin to criticize each other; the lion hates the turtle because he's slow, the turtle hates the elephant because he's big, and so on. When it looks as though disaster will come, the dove restores harmony by appreciating the very qualities in each animal that the other animals have criticized.

INSTRUCTIONS

1. Ask students what are some of the problems that result from diversity (or from people being different). Explain that the story you are going to read shows how diversity created problems for a group of animals. Read *All the Animals Were Angry* by William Wondriska.

2. Discuss the story as suggested below. Distribute Handout 4-5: "It Helps and It Doesn't." Have students complete the handout. With younger children (K-2) simply use the questions on the handout to start a discussion.

3. Explain that when people work together, it helps to have a combination of talents and skills. For example, if students were going to build a treehouse, they might want someone who is good with a saw, someone who is good at climbing, someone who can make a delicious lunch, and someone who has a lot of tools. Ask what five talents and skills they would want in a group of five people who were going to:

- Live with you on a desert island
- Sail to America on the Mayflower
- Set up a lemonade stand
- Go camping in the mountains
- Build a playground on a vacant lot

DISCUSSION QUESTIONS

- Why were the animals angry with each other?
- Have you ever had similar problems with your friends? What did you do?
- How was the dove a peacemaker in this story?
- What are some ways you have been a peacemaker with your friends?

GOING FURTHER

For older students, you can explore similar themes with Natalie Babbitt's *The Search for Delicious*, a delightful book (great for reading aloud) that explores how diversity can lead to conflict and how that can be exploited by unscrupulous people.

Handout 4-5
IT HELPS AND IT DOESN'T

In the book *All the Animals Were Angry,* by William Wondriska, the dove tells each animal that sometimes it is good to be the thing he is. The dove tells the lion that sometimes it is good to be loud. He tells the hippo that sometimes it is good to be fat.

Think about how it might be helpful and not helpful to be different things.

1. When might it be helpful to be loud like the lion?

When might it be a problem to be loud like the lion?

2. When might it be helpful to be tall like the giraffe?

When might it be a problem to be tall like the giraffe?

3. When might it be helpful to be quiet like the snake?

When might it be a problem to be quiet like the snake?

4. When might it be helpful to be smelly like a skunk?

When might it be a problem to be smelly like a skunk?

5. When might it be helpful to be big like the elephant?

When might it be a problem to be big like the elephant?

6. When might it be helpful to be little like the ant?

When might it be a problem to be little like the ant?

6 WHAT'S A STEREOTYPE?

GRADE LEVELS: K-6

OBJECTIVES: To introduce the concept of stereotyping; to analyze stereotypes of a particular ethnic group

SUBJECT AREAS: Social studies, thinking skills

MATERIALS: Optional: pictures of people from the ethnic group you are discussing. The pictures should show people engaged in everyday activities: at work, cooking food, playing with children, washing the car, etc.

INSTRUCTIONS

1. Choose an ethnic group to use as a focal point for the initial discussion. Choose a group not represented in your classroom. For example, the activity that follows is based on stereotypes of Japanese people, but if there are Japanese students in your class, you might want to begin with another group, such as Native Americans.

2. Ask the class: What can you tell me about Japanese people? (Or: If you close your eyes, what mental pictures do you get of Japanese people?) List their ideas on the board.

3. With young children, you might try asking them to draw pictures of Japanese people. They can share their pictures with the group and describe what activities the Japanese person is engaged in.

4. Review the list. Ask: Are all Japanese people like this? Discuss exceptions, emphasizing that people are unique. If possible, show pictures of Japanese people engaged in daily activities. Discuss how the pictures either support or refute the stereotype.

5. Introduce the term "stereotype" as a mental picture of a group of people. Stereotypes lump people together without regard for individual differences.

6. Repeat the activity several times during the year. Use other ethnic groups or any group that is distinctly different, such as elderly people, disabled people, gay people, Russians, Arabs, etc.

7. Another variation is to follow the brainstorming activity with a film about the group you are discussing.

DISCUSSION QUESTIONS

- Where did you learn what you know about Japanese people?
- How do you think Japanese people are different from you? How are they the same as you?
- How might you treat Japanese people based on your stereotypes?
- If you were Japanese, how would you feel about being told you had to be (read part of the list)?

7 DRAW A STEREOTYPE

GRADE LEVELS: 2-4, (5-6)

OBJECTIVES: To explore the concept of stereotypes; to discuss how stereotypes are learned

SUBJECT AREAS: Art, social studies, thinking skills

MATERIALS: Handout 4-7: "Draw a Stereotype"

INSTRUCTIONS

1. Review the meaning of "stereotype": a mental image of a person or group or people that assumes they will look and/or act in a particular way.

2. Distribute Handout 4-7: "Draw a Stereotype." When students have completed their drawings, have them share them with the group and describe the stereotypes they represented.

3. After discussing stereotypes, be sure to spend some time countering the stereotypes this activity raises. For example, if the stereotype of a secretary is a woman typing, ask what other things secretaries do. Also ask if anyone knows a male secretary. If you can arrange it, try to bring into the class some guest speakers who counter these stereotypes: a doctor who is not a white male, a secretary who is male, a father who is a homemaker, etc.

DISCUSSION QUESTIONS

- Where did you learn the stereotypes you identified?
- How might your stereotypes influence how you treat people from this group?
- What are some ways stereotypes hurt you? Other people?
- Can you think of an example of someone in one of these groups who counters the stereotype?

DRAW A STEREOTYPE

In each box, draw a picture of the person named.
The words under the boxes are instructions for pictures you are to draw.

Secretary	**Teacher**
Athlete	**Doctor**
A Mother Working	**A Father Working**

8 THE BIG BAD WOLF

GRADE LEVELS: (K-2), 3-6

OBJECTIVES: To examine the concept of stereotyping by using stereotypes of wolves as an example

Note: This activity takes several days to complete

SUBJECT AREAS: Science, reading, research skills

MATERIALS: Large pieces of newsprint and markers, strips of paper or 3 x 5 cards, reference material on wolves

INSTRUCTIONS

Part 1

1. Have students work in groups of four or five. Designate a recorder and spokesperson in each group. For five minutes, each group should brainstorm a list of attributes about wolves. Ask them to recall everything they ever heard about wolves in stories, animated cartoons, fairy tales, etc.

2. When each group has finished, have the spokesperson read the lists. On the newsprint, record what each group has come up with, even if it repeats what other groups said. Discuss the master list. What conclusions can the class draw about wolves based on the list? Post the list on the wall or bulletin board where it can be seen during the next part of the activity.

Part 2

3. Challenge the class to find out whether or not their list of "facts" about wolves is true. Have them research wolves and bring in as many facts as they can. Each fact should be recorded on a strip of paper and posted. If it contradicts a "fact" on the master list, post it right next to that item.

4. It is also fun for students to bring in more evidence of the stereotypes about wolves, including copies of folk and fairy tales, pictures, popular phrases–even a video of "Peter and the Wolf." Emphasize how much popular support there is for these stereotypes.

DISCUSSION QUESTIONS

- What is the stereotype of wolves?
- Where does that stereotype come from? What kind of "evidence" did you find to support the stereotypes of wolves?
- How different were the facts from the stereotypes?
- How has the stereotype hurt wolves?
- What groups of people often get stereotyped? What "evidence" do other people have for the stereotypes?
- How are people hurt by stereotypes?

GOING FURTHER

Once students have completed this activity, have them conduct a poll to find out what stereotypes other people have about wolves. An interesting experiment is for them to try to convince people of the facts about wolves. Have students report back on their experiences confronting the prejudice against wolves. What did they learn about how to confront people's stereotypes and prejudices?

9 WHAT IS PREJUDICE? (THE SNEETCHES)

GRADE LEVELS: K-6

OBJECTIVES: To introduce the concepts of prejudice and discrimination by using *The Sneetches* by Dr. Seuss; to explore how prejudice is learned; to discuss the negative effects of prejudice and discrimination

SUBJECT AREAS: Reading, language arts, social studies, thinking skills

MATERIALS: *The Sneetches* by Dr. Seuss (Random House/1961).

Summary

The Star-Belly Sneetches think that they are better than the Plain-Belly Sneetches. But once the Plain-Belly Sneetches learn how to place stars on their bellies, things begin to get confused. Soon Sneetches are adding and removing stars as fast as they can. How is anyone to know who's better than whom?

INSTRUCTIONS

1. Begin by asking the class: What is prejudice? Record several responses on the board. Explain that you are going to read aloud a story with which some of them may be familiar. The story will help them understand what prejudice is and how it affects people.

2. Read the story aloud (or use film/video version). Discuss as suggested below.

DISCUSSION QUESTIONS

- What stereotypes did the Star-Belly Sneetches have?
- The Star-Belly Sneetches were not born prejudiced. How did they learn prejudice?
- In what ways are the Sneetches like people?
- Are there groups of people that other people are prejudiced against?
- How did prejudice hurt the Plain-Belly Sneetches? How did it hurt the Star-Belly Sneetches?
- What are some real-life examples of prejudice and discrimination?

10 ALL KIDS

GRADE LEVELS: 3-6

OBJECTIVES: To personalize the concept of stereotypes by examining generalizations about children

SUBJECT AREAS: Social studies

MATERIALS: Chalkboard and chalk

INSTRUCTIONS

1. Review the concept of generalizing. Ask the class to think about generalizations adults make about kids. Have them complete the sentence stub, "All kids --."

2. On the board, make two tally charts, one headed *Positive* and *Negative* and the other headed *True* and *False*.

3. Have the students read their generalizations aloud. Have the class decide if each generalization is true or false, positive or negative.

4. Discuss the results, making sure the students understand that generalizing is not inherently bad, but that problems arise when generalizations aren't rooted in fact. Discuss how generalizations can lead to stereotypes.

DISCUSSION QUESTIONS

- Why do people make generalizations?
- How could generalizations be harmful?
- How might they be helpful?
- How might generalizations fuel conflict?
- What could you do if you hear someone making an inaccurate generalization?
- How do generalizations lead to stereotypes?

From *Creative Conflict Resolution* by *William J. Kreidler. Scott, Foresman and Co., 1984, pp. 167-168.*

‖ M AND S
AUTO REPAIR

GRADE LEVELS: 3-6

OBJECTIVES: To identify stereotypes based on sex; to understand the feelings of people who experience sexism

SUBJECT AREAS: Language arts, reading

MATERIALS: Handout 4-11a: "M and S Auto Repair," one per student; Handout 4-11b: "Roles for Marcie and Jim," one per pair

INSTRUCTIONS

1. Have students read the handout "M and S Auto Repair" and answer the questions at the end. Discuss the questions together as a class.

2. Tell students that they'll do a role play. Tell them that five months have gone by. After much hard work and after fighting opposition to their idea from many people, Marcie and Sonia have opened the M and S Auto Repair Shop.

3. Ask two students to do a sample role play in front of the class. Remind students they must become the person whose role they are playing. Even if they don't agree with the role, they should get into the feelings. Give the two volunteers their part of the handout, "Roles for Marcie and Jim." After they've read it, check with them privately to make sure they understand their roles well. Tell the students that since this is a sample, you will interrupt after two minutes, even though the role play may not be over.

4. Now divide all the students into pairs, give each child a role, and begin role playing simultaneously. After about three or four minutes stop them. Have students exchange roles.

From Open Minds to Equality by Nancy Schniedwind and Ellen Davidson. © 1983, pp. 90-93, 107-110. Reprinted by permission of Prentice Hall, Inc., Englewood Cliffs, New Jersey.

Handout 4-11a
M AND S AUTO REPAIR

Marcie and Sonia are two women in their middle twenties who live in the town of North Jefferson. Both graduated from high school with a strong background in science, math, and auto mechanics. Since then they have worked in Bob Miller's auto repair shop. By now they have had seven years' experience on the job. They have excellent reputations as auto mechanics.

Marcie and Sonia have all the skills they need to open their own shop, M and S Auto Repair. The women have saved the money they need to get their business going.

Sonia called the owner of a local garage to ask if it was for rent. The owner said, "Sure, lady. Have your husband come over any time. I'm eager to rent."

Sonia went to the garage later that afternoon. The owner said, "Where's your husband?" When she told him she wanted to rent it for herself, he laughed in her face. "What? *You* want to rent the garage! What a joke."

"I'm not married. I'm an auto mechanic, and here is my down payment."

"Look, lady, I'm not renting this to you. I'll lose money. You'll never be able to pay your rent. Nobody in this town will come to a garage run by women. Give up your pie-in-the-sky idea."

1. Describe how you would feel if you were Sonia.

2. How does the garage owner show prejudice toward Sonia?

3. What are the stereotypes about women that the garage owner has?

4. How do these stereotypes hurt Marcie and Sonia?

5. How will these stereotypes hurt the residents of North Jefferson?

Handout 4-11b
ROLES FOR MARCIE AND JIM

MARCIE

You are very confident in your abilities as an auto mechanic. You successfully fixed at least 400 cars when you worked in your past job. You received very few complaints. In fact, your boss told you that you are one of the most skilled auto repair workers that he has ever employed.

In the role play, try to convince the customer to leave his car at M and S for you to fix.

JIM

You read about a new garage that is opening in town, M and S Auto Repair. You're so pleased, since mechanics at the other shops have never successfully fixed your car. You call and make an appointment to leave your car. When you walk in, you see a woman. You're shocked. You don't want a woman repairing your car.

In the role play, try to find a way to get out of leaving your car at M and S Auto Repair.

1. Describe your feelings as you play Marcie.

2. Describe your feelings as you play Jim.

3. In the end did Jim leave his car or not? What arguments influenced his decision?

4. What are other stereotypes some people have about women? How do these stereotypes hurt women?

5. What can we do to counteract stereotypes that hurt people because of their sex?

156

12 WE ALL LOSE

GRADE LEVELS: 4-6

OBJECTIVES: To identify how stereotypes, prejudice, and discrimination harm everyone

SUBJECT AREAS: Reading, language arts

MATERIALS: Handout 4-12a: "We All Lose," two per group; Handout 4-12b: "Situation Cards," one set per group, cut and mounted on cards; paper and pencils

INSTRUCTIONS

1. Divide students into heterogeneous groups of three to six. Give each group copies of the situation cards and handout "We All Lose," paper and pencils, card stock, and pens. Review definitions of prejudice and stereotypes and go over several cards as a whole class to give students the idea.

2. Students read cards aloud. For each one, they discuss what stereotype or prejudice it shows, why they think people might have that stereotype, and what harm it causes. Each group picks four cards and fills in the handout on them. Come together as a class for the discussion questions.

3. After discussion, have students take the card stock and cut themselves four cards of the same size. Then have them create new cards describing situations typical of their school or lives. For each card, they make a handout entry. In that way they will have to pick a stereotype or a type of prejudice and think it through clearly.

4. Share these with the whole class, perhaps having each group pass its stack on to another group. Finally, as a group, discuss the new cards.

5. You can also use these cards as part of a board game. Just add "lose a turn," "go back a space," or "take another turn" to the end of the card. Students can create a regular pathway game board. The theme should be connected with equality. This stack of cards can form the basis for the "luck" cards.

DISCUSSION QUESTIONS

- How did the person stereotyped lose in the situations? Discuss one at a time.
- How did the person stereotyping lose out?
- What can you do to unlearn these stereotypes and to help yourself not to learn more?

GOING FURTHER

Berries Goodman by Emily Cheney Neville (Harper & Row, 1965) is a straightforward and powerful story about some very real children and their families experiencing antisemitism.

From Open Minds to Equality by Nancy Schniedwind and Ellen Davidson. © 1983, pp. 90-93, 107-110. Reprinted by permission of Prentice Hall, Inc., Englewood Cliffs, New Jersey.

Handout 4-12a
WE ALL LOSE

- ✂ - - - - - - - -

Card Number _____

Stereotype
    or
Prejudice _____

Harm caused by stereotype or prejudice to *each* person in the situation

- ✂ - - - - - - - -

Card Number _____

Stereotype
    or
Prejudice _____

Harm caused by stereotype or prejudice to *each* person in the situation

- ✂ - - - - - - - -

Card Number _____

Stereotype
    or
Prejudice _____

Harm caused by stereotype or prejudice to *each* person in the situation

- ✂ - - - - - - - -

Card Number _____

Stereotype
    or
Prejudice _____

Harm caused by stereotype or prejudice to *each* person in the situation

- ✂ - - - - - - - -

Handout 4-12b
SITUATION CARDS

- ✂ - - - - - - - - - -

1. Joe gets hit in the eye with a baseball. He starts to cry. The other guys begin to make fun of him. You feel bad for him, but chime in with the other guys and say, "Don't be a sissy."

- ✂ - - - - - - - - - -

2. You want to build a pen for your dog. The only person around tall enough to help you is Ramona. You say, "I need a boy to help me." You don't get help and the dog runs away.

- ✂ - - - - - - - - - -

3. Some Latino students ask you to join their group to do a math project. You think they're not so smart, so you join another group. Their group gets an A, yours doesn't.

- ✂ - - - - - - - - - -

4. You are a fine dancer, and would like to take up ballet. You're afraid the other guys will make fun of you. You give up your plan, lots of good exercise, and a possible career.

- ✂ - - - - - - - - - -

5. You fall and think you've broken your ankle. A black woman who is a doctor offers to look at it. You don't trust her so you refuse. You end up lying there in pain for hours before someone else comes to help you.

- ✂ - - - - - - - - - -

6. Joan's family doesn't have much money. They live in a different neighborhood from yours. She invites you to her birthday party. You don't go because you think her house will be messy and dirty. You miss a great time and a spotless house.

- ✂ - - - - - - - - - -

7. You missed the bus and need a ride to school. Ms. Mendez is 82. She offers to drive you. You think she'll drive off the road. You kill your feet walking four miles to school.

- ✂ - - - - - - - - - -

8. Your younger sister keeps calling her friend a "wild Indian." She shoots him again and again with a toy gun. You don't correct her.

13 STATUS CARD GAME

GRADE LEVELS: 3-6

OBJECTIVES: To initiate a discussion of power and status; to explore how people are treated according to their power

SUBJECT AREAS: Social studies, social skills

MATERIALS: Deck of ordinary playing cards with the face cards and aces removed

INSTRUCTIONS

1. Begin the lesson by asking students to define what status is (or what it means to be popular). Allow for a short discussion. Then tell students that they are about to play a game that explores power and status.

2. Divide the class into two groups of equal size (up to eighteen students in a group). Have one group stand around the edges of an open space, and have the other group stand in the center. Explain to students in the center that they are going to act out a certain social situation, and to the students on the outside that they are going to observe. Plan ahead of time what social situation to use: a party, bus ride to school, playground, rehearsal for a show—whatever is a known social situation to the age group. Also explain that you are about to assign them a role using the numbered playing cards. Holding the cards face down in front of you, pass them out face down to students. *Be sure to tell them not to look at their card.*

3. While you are passing out the cards explain that you are using only numbered cards, and that a low card (a 2, 3, or 4) means that the person has a low status (or is "unpopular"), and that a high card (an 8, 9, or 10) denotes high status. Remind them that you are doing it randomly; you have no idea what number they are receiving. As you finish, take a card for yourself and, without looking at it, hold it up to your forehead face out. Everyone can see the number, but you don't know what number you have. Again reminding them to not look at their own card, tell them that they are supposed to react to or treat people like a 2 or a 5 or a 9, according to the card the other person has on his or her forehead.

4. Once everyone understands how to interpret the cards, have them put their cards up on their forehead. If the scene is a party, they can mill about to interact with each other. They could also get onto an imaginary bus single file for a field trip (set chairs up in rows to mimic seats) and then negotiate who will sit with whom. Other interactive social situations are possible. But whatever the situation, encourage them to interact according to each other's status.

5. Allow the group to interact for a couple minutes. Remind observers to note who interacts with whom, and to see if any groups or cliques form.

6. Stop the scene. But immediately ask participants to *not* look at their cards. Then ask them to place themselves on an imaginary line across the room according to what status they think they are: high-status people at one end, low-status people at another, middle-status people in the middle. Encourage them to change places if they think they are lower or higher than someone next to them.

7. Once the line has stabilized–with cards still on foreheads, and starting at one end–ask the first student what number he or she thinks he or she is and why. After the student answers, he or she may look at the card. Go all the way down the line, giving each a chance to answer and look at the card.

8. Next, ask the observers if they have any comments. Discuss. Then replay the game with the groups switching places.

DISCUSSION QUESTIONS

- How did it feel to be a 9 or 10? How did you know you were a high number? How did people treat you?
- How did it feel to be a 1 or 2 or 3? How did you know you were a low number? How did people treat you?
- How did it feel to be in the middle (4, 5, 6, 7)? How did you know you were a middle number? How did people treat you?
- Did any high-number people try to be friends with low-number people? Tell us what happened.
- Did any low-number people try to be friends with high-number people? What happened?

Game from Stephen DiMenna, Minneapolis, Minnesota.

Chapter Five:
PEACE AND ENEMIES

INTRODUCTION

There is a story, perhaps apocryphal, of an aide approaching Abraham Lincoln when he was pardoning Southerners after the Civil War. "But Mr. Lincoln," protested the aide, "don't you want to eliminate your enemies?" Lincoln replied, "Is that not what I do when I make them my friends?"

We have enemies for many reasons. Some of our enemies are the result of fears and prejudices we've been taught. Sometimes enemies are created to help define us as individuals or as a group. And sometimes people or groups of people really do hate us or want to hurt us. Sometimes our enemies are the result of all three of these.

People have asked me, "Should we talk with children about enemies? Won't it just put the idea in their heads?" Research indicates that children develop the concept of enemies very early. I believe they develop it on their own, without needing to be exposed to it. In fact, they will have enemies in their lives, and I am more concerned about how they learn to deal with enemies.

As with conflict, the most common responses to enemies seem to be violence and avoidance. But there are many ways that people have dealt with enemies and with evil actions on the part of others, including befriending enemies and nonviolent resistance to evil actions. We owe it to children to expose them to these possibilities as well.

The first group of activities (numbers 1-6) deals directly with the concept of enemies: how they develop and what we can do about them. The second group (numbers 7-11) deals with propaganda and its relationship to enemies. The third group (numbers 12-14) addresses nonviolent ways to confront evil.

Teaching Considerations

It is helpful for students to have an understanding of the vocabulary and concepts of stereotyping and prejudice before they explore the concept of enemies.

- The purpose of these activities is to explore why we have enemies and how our thinking about enemies can be clouded by stereotypes, prejudices, and propaganda. You may also find it helpful to refer back to the concept of escalation in chapter 3, "Peace and Conflict." The enemy, like the conflict, may be real, but other factors may contribute unnecessarily to escalating the feeling of enmity, making the relationship worse than it needs to be.

- Sometimes enemies become friends and sometimes they don't. While it is important that children understand this possibility, it is also important to acknowledge that it will not always occur. Emphasize exploring many possibilities and discuss how to make decisions in such matters.

- Children may resist trying to understand the point of view of the enemy. Developmentally this is understandable; children like their bad guys to be bad and their good guys to be good. But, as was discussed earlier, taking another person's perspective is both a skill and a value we want to promote. After all, understanding the point of view of the enemy does not mean you agree with or approve of his or her actions. To the extent that your students are able to understand another's point of view, encourage them and give them opportunities to do so.

Connecting to Larger Issues

Help students monitor current events with an eye toward identifying people and groups that are enemies. Students will be able to see in the behavior of groups and nations much of the same enemy behavior that individuals exhibit. Discuss what forms this behavior takes and how it affects relations between the enemies.

ENEMIES
WEB CHART

GRADE LEVELS: K-6

OBJECTIVES: To explore the concept of enemies by brainstorming a web chart; to look at some of the complexities involved in the concept of "enemies"

SUBJECT AREAS: Social studies, language arts

MATERIALS: Large pieces of paper and crayons or markers

INSTRUCTIONS

1. Have students work in groups of three or four. Supply each group with a large piece of paper and crayons or markers. Have students choose one group member to write "enemy" in the center of the paper and circle it.

2. Have the group members take turns adding to the web their associations with the word "enemy," as follows:

frightening —— **ENEMY** —— bad

dangerous   mean

Encourage students to include feeling words, not just cognitive associations.

3. Post the web charts where all can see. Allow students time to examine the charts other groups created.

DISCUSSION QUESTIONS

- What are the similarities and differences among the charts?
- Can you have these same associations with a friend; can a friend be mean? Frightening?
- What's the difference between a friend being mean (or kind or noisy or secretive) and an enemy being the same?

2 ROLE-PLAYING FRIENDS AND ENEMIES

GRADE LEVELS: K-6

OBJECTIVES: To examine, through role playing, how people treat friends and enemies; to experiment with different ways to treat enemies

SUBJECT AREAS: Drama, social skills, thinking skills

MATERIALS: None

INSTRUCTIONS

1. Have students pick partners and then stand facing each other for the role plays. One student should be A and the other should be B. A and B are good friends.

2. Choose a "30-Second Role Play" from those below. Read the situation aloud, then give the starting signal. Time the role plays for thirty seconds.

30-Second Role Plays

A cuts ahead of **B** in line. How does **B** react?
A calls **B** a jerk. How does **B** react?
B asks **A** to play a game. How does **A** react?
B borrows **A**'s crayons and accidentally breaks them. How does **A** react?
A tripped **B** on the way to gym. How does **B** react?
B has cookies for snack. How does **A** react?

3. Now repeat the role plays with A and B as enemies.

4. Discuss the role play as suggested below, adding your own observations.

DISCUSSION QUESTIONS

• Do we react differently to friends than enemies? In what ways? Why?
• Do we have to treat enemies with meanness even if we don't like them?

3 DRAWING FRIENDS AND ENEMIES

GRADE LEVELS: K-6

OBJECTIVES: To examine, through drawing, the differences in how we perceive friends, enemies, and strangers

SUBJECT AREAS: Art, language arts

Note: This activity takes two sessions

MATERIALS: Three sheets 8 ½ x 11 drawing paper for each student, tape, chalkboard and chalk

INSTRUCTIONS

Part 1

1. Distribute three sheets of drawing paper to each student. Explain that they will be drawing three pictures. One will be a picture of what a stranger looks like. Another will be a picture of what a friend looks like. The third will be a picture of what an enemy looks like. They will NOT label their pictures.

2. Have students draw their pictures. The picture of a friend should not be an actual friend, but instead an imaginary or generic friendly person.

3. When all the students have finished, collect the drawings.

Part 2

4. Divide the chalkboard into three sections. Label one section "Friends," another section "Strangers," and the third "Enemies."

5. Distribute the drawings from Part 1 at random. Each student should receive three drawings that are not his or her own. Ask students to decide what they think each drawing represents, a friend, an enemy, or a stranger.

6. Invite students to tape the drawings on the board under the appropriate label.

7. With younger students, simply have them fold a sheet of drawing paper in half and draw one picture of a friend and one of an enemy.

DISCUSSION QUESTIONS

- Was it easy or difficult to figure out which drawing was which?
- What did friends tend to look like? Enemies?
- Are enemies always mean looking?
- Are friends always nice?

4 A TOAD FOR TUESDAY

GRADE LEVELS: K-3

OBJECTIVES: To examine ways enemies can become friends; to practice adopting other perspectives

SUBJECT AREAS: Reading, language arts

MATERIALS: *A Toad For Tuesday* by Russell Erickson (Lothrop, Lee and Shepard, 1973)

Summary

One winter day, Warton the toad and his brother Morton are enjoying Morton's delicious Beetle Brittle. Warton decides to take some to their Aunt Toolia. Despite his brother's warnings, Warton is determined to make the dangerous journey on a set of skis he makes just for the occasion.

Warton's journey is uneventful until he is captured by an owl, who promises him that he is going to eat him as a birthday treat on the following Tuesday. How Warton copes with this threat to his life and befriends the owl is the focus of the rest of the book.

INSTRUCTIONS

1. Read aloud or have students read *A Toad for Tuesday* by Russell Erickson. Discuss the book as suggested below, touching on such issues as how enemies become friends, how trust is built up between people, and how trust is broken.

2. The dialogue on pages 22-46 brings up many issues that are at the heart of *A Toad for Tuesday*. Have a group of three or four students use the dialogue on those pages to create a play. They should include a narrator who will introduce the situation, but encourage them to leave the play open-ended. Audiences can then guess what they think the ending of the book is.

3. In real life an owl and a toad, like many animals, are natural enemies; they are predator and prey. In fiction, of course, such enemies can become friends. Have students choose a pair of animals that are natural enemies. Next, have them write stories that show how the two animals learn to trust each other, become friends, or at least learn how to live peaceably together. Some possibilities are a chicken and a fox, a cat and a bluejay, a robin and a worm.

DISCUSSION QUESTIONS

- Why do you think that George didn't have any friends?
- Since Warton didn't believe that George would let him go, why do you think he was so friendly to George?
- How do you think George felt when he found Warton's escape ladder?
- Have you ever had an enemy you learned to trust and maybe even to like? Tell what happened.

5 THE ISLAND OF THE SKOG

GRADE LEVELS: K-3, (4-6)

OBJECTIVES: To explore how assumptions affect our behavior

SUBJECT AREAS: Reading

MATERIALS: *The Island of the Skog* by Steven Kellogg (Dial Press, 1973)

Summary

Frustrated by the dangers of urban living, a group of mice set sail on a model ship to search for a more peaceful place to live. They finally land on the Island of the Skog, a place with only one inhabitant–the Skog. Judging by its enormous footprint, the mice assume the Skog is a terrible threat to them, and they invent various ways to intimidate and/or capture him. The Skog turns out to be a mild-mannered little creature who is as frightened by the mice as they are of him.

INSTRUCTIONS

1. Read the story aloud or have students read it themselves. Discuss the story as suggested below, touching on such issues as assumptions about other people and how they affect our behavior, points of view, and how we choose to behave toward enemies and friends.

2. Point out that Louise thought the mice should approach the Skog with a present to show that they wanted to be friends. Have students write and illustrate (or, for younger students, dictate and illustrate) how the story might have ended if that had happened.

3. Have students draw how the following episodes looked from the Skog's point of view: the boat firing at the island, the mice looking at the big footprint, the mice making a bear trap, and the mice planning a honey trap. Discuss how he felt watching these things.

4. Older students can rewrite the story from the Skog's point of view.

DISCUSSION QUESTIONS

- Why did Bouncer say they had to fire the cannon? Do you agree?
- The mice had a choice between being friendly and being hostile. What were the consequences of their choosing to be hostile?
- What evidence did the mice think they had that the Skog was dangerous? What evidence did they ignore?
- What did the Skog mean when he said it is better to be alone than to be afraid? Do you agree?
- Have you ever been afraid of someone and found out that they were afraid of you? Tell what happened.

6 VILLAINS ARE HUMAN TOO

GRADE LEVELS: 2-6

OBJECTIVES: To develop personal histories for supervillains; to examine why enemies are seen as entirely evil

SUBJECT AREAS: Language arts, thinking skills

MATERIALS: None

INSTRUCTIONS

1. Brainstorm with the children a list of the worst "bad guys" they can think of. They may name a few real people, but it is more likely their examples will come from movies, television, and fictional literature. If you aren't familiar with names the children suggest, encourage them to say a few words about who the character is and what he or she does that is so evil.

2. Pick one of the characters who seems to be well known to most of the children, and discuss him or her with the class, focusing on parts of the character's life other than evil deeds.

3. Some questions you might ask are:

• Where was the villain born? What day is the villain's birthday? What was his or her first word? What were his parents like? What games did he or she like as a baby?
• When the villain was a child, what was his or her favorite food? Dessert? Toy? Game? Color? Sport? Book? TV show? Movie? (Add other questions to elicit details of childhood likes and dislikes.)
• Where did the villain go to school? What was his or her favorite school subject? Did the villain bring lunch or buy a school lunch? What did he or she eat for lunch? What did he or she do at recess? (Add other questions to elicit details of early school experience.)
• Imagine a time when the villain got hurt as a child. What was he or she doing and what happened? Did he or she cry? (Encourage children to recognize that all of us cry when we get badly hurt.) Did he or she have to go to the hospital? Get stitches? Get a cast or a bandage? How was his or her activity limited while he or she was healing? Did his or her parents give him or her any treats to make up for the pain? (Ask other questions to elicit details about a time the villain was most vulnerable and hurt.)

This activity was suggested by Susan Jones.

- Think of a time when the villain was an especially "good boy" or "good girl." What did he or she do? Who appreciated it? Was he or she rewarded for good behavior? (Ask other questions to elicit details of childhood good behavior.)
- Imagine a time when the villain was proud; when he or she was frightened; when he or she was lonely; when he or she had a lot of fun; when his or her feelings got hurt. Imagine his or her first day of school; his or her fifth (or seventh or ninth) birthday party; his or her first pet; his or her favorite vacation. (Add more questions to elicit details of childhood experiences the children can readily identify with.)
- People sometimes become "mean" when something happens to them that makes them feel bad, when they're treated unfairly, or when their needs aren't met. What might have happened to the villain to make him or her become mean? (This will take some careful and sensitive direction to help children construct a possible set of reasons for the development of the character's evil streak.)

DISCUSSION QUESTIONS

- What makes someone a "bad guy"?
- Why do people think enemies are all bad?
- What's the difference between someone who's all bad and someone who does bad things?

GOING FURTHER

Follow-up activities might include having the children construct a past and a full personality for another supervillain of their choosing (if you sense that they haven't used all their ideas on the group discussion just completed); drawing pictures or cartoons of different episodes and features of his or her life; writing stories about some of these features; role-playing episodes from the villain's life; and conducting a make-believe interview with him or her.

7 ENEMIES THEN AND NOW

GRADE LEVELS: 4-6

OBJECTIVES: To examine how enemies of the United States have changed over the years

SUBJECT AREAS: Social studies, research skills

MATERIALS: Handout 5-7: "Friends and Enemies, Then and Now," world map

INSTRUCTIONS

1. Begin by having the class brainstorm a list of all the countries they can think of that have, at one time or another, been enemies of the United States. When the list is complete, ask: Which of these countries is now a friend? Place a star next to each one.

2. Distribute Handout 5-7 : "Friends and Enemies, Then and Now." Go over the items, locating the appropriate countries on the map.

DISCUSSION QUESTIONS

• Are there any countries that have never been enemies of the US?
• Are there any that have never been friends (or allies)?
• What does it mean to say a country is our "friend"?
• Why do you think so many countries have been both enemies and friends?
• What do countries do that make them enemies of each other?
• What can countries who are enemies do to become friends?

Handout 5-7
FRIENDS AND ENEMIES, THEN AND NOW

Nations that were enemies of the United States have become friends, and nations that were friends of the United States have become enemies. Here are some examples:

1775 The British were our friends, the French were our enemies. (It was the French and Indian War.)

1776 The French were our friends, the British were our enemies. (It was the American Revolution.)

1799 The French were our enemies again. (There were sea battles with France.)

1812 The French were our friends again. The British were our enemies. (It was the War of 1812.)

1914 The Japanese and the Russians were our friends. (It was the beginning of World War I. They were our allies.)

1914 The British and the French were our friends. Austrians and Germans were our enemies. (It was the beginning of World War I.)

1918 Italy was our friend. (It became our ally in World War I.)

1935 Italy was our enemy. (Italy invaded Ethiopia.)

1939 The British and the French were our friends. The Russians and the Germans were our enemies. (It was the beginning of World War II.)

1941 The Russians were our friends. (Russia became an ally in World War II.)

1947 The Chinese were our friends. The Russians were now our enemies.

1955 The West Germans and Japanese were our friends. The Russians, Chinese, and East Germans were our enemies.

Who are our friends and enemies now?

8 PROPAGANDA TECHNIQUES

GRADE LEVELS: 4-6

OBJECTIVES: To introduce basic propaganda techniques; to identify examples of these techniques

SUBJECT AREAS: Reading, social studies, thinking skills

MATERIALS: Handout 5-8: "Propaganda Techniques," magazines

INSTRUCTIONS

1. Begin by supplying students with magazines and asking them to clip a variety of advertisements. Select clippings to illustrate the following propaganda techniques:

- Bandwagon–everybody's doing it
- Testimonials–"authorities" or celebrities vouching for a product
- Selection of facts–using only the facts that support the product and omitting those that don't
- Repetition–saying it again and again
- Emotional appeals–playing on fear, pity, status, pride, hunger, etc.
- Stereotyping–presenting images of "good" mothers, fathers, children, etc.

Depending on the age of your students, some of these propaganda techniques will be easier to grasp than others. The Bandwagon, for example, is easy for almost any age to recognize, while Selection of Facts if more difficult. The important thing at this point is that the techniques be introduced and explained; students will get more practice in identification later.

2. Have students work in groups and classify the advertisements according to the categories above. They will quickly notice that some ads use several approaches at once and that others seem not to fit in any category. Have the students set the latter aside. When they have finished, read these to the class and discuss how the advertisement is trying to influence them.

3. For homework, have students find examples of TV commercials that fit these categories. (This may be the most popular homework you assign all year!) Discuss how the techniques are enhanced or changed by TV.

4. With older students (grades 5 and 6), you can help them see how these techniques are used in politics. Tape a presidential speech on audio- or videotape and note those sections that illustrate obvious attempts to influence the listener. Play the tape for students in short sections (or read a newspaper transcript of the speech), and ask them to identify any propaganda techniques being used.

DISCUSSION QUESTIONS

- Why do people attempt to influence others?
- Are advertisements true? (It should be stressed here that technically they are true, but the truth is often presented in such a way as to make it more attractive.)
- Is it right to try to influence others? (Stress that this is a value judgment students must make based on how the influencing is done.)
- Why is it important to understand how propaganda techniques work?

Handout 5-8:
PROPAGANDA TECHNIQUES

Bandwagon

(Everybody's doing it!)

Testimonial

Authorities or celebrities vouching for a product

Selection of Facts

Using only facts that support the product or argument leaving out the rest

Repetition

Saying something over and over again

Emotional Appeals

Playing on fear, pity, status, pride, guilt, etc

Stereotyping

Presenting "good" mothers, fathers, children, etc. or "bad" people

9 USING PROPAGANDA

GRADE LEVELS: 4-6

OBJECTIVES: To reinforce children's understanding of propaganda techniques

SUBJECT AREAS: Language arts, reading, thinking skills

MATERIALS: Handout 5-9: "Propaganda Techniques" from Activity 5-8

INSTRUCTIONS

This can be used as a follow-up to Activity 5-8. Students will try to use the propaganda techniques they have just studied.

1. Have students invent a fictitious character.

2. Using one or more of the propaganda techniques in Activity 5-8, they should write an advertisement "selling" this person. It can be for a particular job or just a popularity contest.

3. Now have them write an ad attacking this same character, again using the previously mentioned techniques.

DISCUSSION QUESTIONS

- Did you think your campaigns were persuasive? Why?
- How did it feel to "switch sides" in your ad campaign?
- What more did you learn about how propaganda works?
- What were the different feelings involved in using influence as compared to being influenced (in the previous activity)?

10 CREATE AN ENEMY

GRADE LEVELS: 4-6

OBJECTIVES: To examine how propaganda is used to encourage enmity

SUBJECT AREAS: Language arts, thinking skills, social studies

MATERIALS: Handout 5-10a: "Background on Overton and Underton," Handout 5-10b: "Create an Enemy," and, for reference, Handout 5-8: "Propaganda Techniques" from Activity 5-8

INSTRUCTIONS

1. Divide students into groups of four and assign roles:

• Taskmaster–keeps group on task and gets materials
• Recorder–writes down what the group decides
• Reader–reads materials and makes sure everyone understands
• Spokesperson–speaks for the group

2. Explain the task, which is to create an enemy. Each group is Overton, a nation that lies next to Underton. Overton and Underton have peacefully coexisted for a hundred years. Now, as leaders in the country of Overton, you want to convince the citizens that Underton is really an enemy, even though nothing between your two nations has really changed. The task is to develop a plan to portray Underton as an enemy. The plans should include written and visual materials, such as posters, billboards, TV commercials, leaflets, or speeches. There should also be a written plan explaining how these will be used.

3. Review the techniques learned in Activity 5-8: "Propaganda Techniques." The students should use some of these techniques in planning their enemy-creating campaigns.

4. Allow thirty minutes to an hour for students to formulate their plans. Then, over the next week, give the groups time to create materials to use in their plans, such as posters, commercials, etc.

5. At the end, have the groups share their plans and sample materials.

DISCUSSION QUESTIONS

- How are your enemy plans similar to the way nations (or groups) treat enemies? How are they different?
- Why are some nations enemies? Why do you think nations create such propaganda about their enemies?
- What are some examples of groups within the country that think of each other as enemies? How do they use propaganda?
- How does propaganda make it more complicated to deal with enemies?
- What are some of the ways groups (or nations) that are enemies can become friends?

Handout 5-10a
BACKGROUND ON OVERTON AND UNDERTON

OVERTON is located in the northern part of a continent. Some of its biggest industries are making cars, medical equipment, and electronic equipment. Overton also has great agricultural areas. It produces much of the world's wheat and corn. Oats do not grow well in Overton. It also processes much of the food grown in Underton.

Overton doesn't manufacture much paper or cloth, even though the trees and plants needed for these products are grown in Overton. Many people in Overton are out of work these days. Many factories have closed because the things they manufactured are now made in other countries.

■

UNDERTON is located to the south of Overton. It is a bigger country in area, but has a smaller population than Overton. Most people have jobs. Many fruits and vegetables are grown in Underton. Until recently they were shipped to Overton to be frozen or canned. Now Underton has started to process the food it grows.

Oats grow well in Underton, and in the past few years people all over the world have begun to eat more oats, because they are so nutritious. Near the border of Overton and Underton are paper mills and textile factories. Wood and plants are grown in Overton and shipped to Underton to be made into paper and cloth. Underton is able to make paper and cloth more cheaply than any other country.

Handout 5-10b
CREATE AN ENEMY

In what ways is Overton better off than Underton?

In what ways is Underton better off than Overton?

How could you use these facts as part of your propaganda campaign?

What are some facts about Underton that you could use in a propaganda campaign against it?

What are some facts you would leave out?

What are some very emotional words you could use to describe Underton?

THE BULLY OF BARKHAM STREET

GRADE LEVELS: 3-6

OBJECTIVES: To explore reasons why people bully others; to practice adopting the perspective of an enemy

SUBJECT AREAS: Reading, language arts, thinking skills

MATERIALS: *The Bully of Barkham St.* by Mary Stolz (Harper & Row, 1963)

Summary

Eleven-year-old Martin Hastings is a bully. He ignores his teacher, talks back to adults, picks on kids smaller than he, and hates everyone in the world except his dog Rufus. Martin is in trouble at home and school, and friendless in the neighborhood, but his troubles become even worse when his parents get rid of Rufus. Eventually, after many mishaps, Martin realizes that he must change. He begins the long, slow process of improving himself and his reputation in the neighborhood.

INSTRUCTIONS

1. Read or have students read *The Bully of Barkham St.* by Mary Stolz. Before reading, discuss with students their impressions of what a bully is, why bullies act the way they do, and how people react to bullies. Spend some time encouraging the students to tell you how they think bullies think and feel about their actions. Then explain that you (or they) will be reading a book told from the point of view of a bully.

2. Have students pretend to be Martin at the end of the book. Ask them to write letters to Martin at the beginning of the book, giving him advice on how to change his life and his reputation.

3. Have students list five adjectives that describe both Martin and themselves. Next, have them list two problems that both they and Martin have in common. Have them share their results and discuss ways in which we are all a little bit like Martin in the way we feel, if not the way we act.

DISCUSSION QUESTIONS

- Why did Martin like to pick on kids that were smaller than he was?
- Martin made several attempts to be nice to Edward. Why didn't they work?
- What does it mean that Martin often felt like an outsider?
- How did Martin's daydreams change as he changed? What do his daydreams tell about him?
- Tell about a time when you felt misunderstood the way Martin did.

12 RESCUE IN DENMARK: A Choral Reading

GRADE LEVELS: 3-6

OBJECTIVES: To learn about the rescue of Danish Jews from the Nazis during World War II; to explore motivations for nonviolent resistance

SUBJECT AREAS: Social studies, reading

MATERIALS: The enclosed reading, cut into appropriate parts. The activity is designed with choral reading parts for twenty students. If you have more than twenty students, longer readings can be divided into two parts. The reading is divided into four sections: Background, parts 1-4; Warning, parts 5-9; Hiding, parts 10-15; and Escape, parts 16-20.

INSTRUCTIONS

1. Before distributing roles, take time to discuss anti-Semitism and the Nazi persecution of the Jews during World War II. Draw upon student knowledge. Begin when you believe students have a clear historical context for the reading.

2. Divide students into the four basic groups (Background, Warning, Hiding, Escape). Pass out readings. While you might want to help students with pronunciation of Danish names, remind them that accurate pronunciation is not important for the activity. Don't belabor it. Ask students to read their parts silently, then pair up in twos or threes to practice reading aloud. Tell them that their goal is to read in a clear, strong voice and with feeling. They are recreating feeling in the classroom.

3. When students are prepared, bring them together. If possible, sit in a circle, in proper numerical sequence. Reader 1 stands, reads his or her part, and others follow in order.

DISCUSSION QUESTIONS

- How did you feel being part of this choral reading?
- What words would you use to describe the actions of the Danes?
- What risks did they take in helping the Jews?
- How do you feel about the actions of the Danes?
- What do you think you would have done if you were a Dane who wasn't a Jew? Why?
- How does anti-Semitism exist in our own society? What can we do to deal with that?

• The action of the Danes is an example of many people working together in nonviolent resistance to oppression. What do you think of this alternative to military power? What are other examples of the use of this alternative? Cite examples from American history and from the history of other countries.

GOING FURTHER

Lois Lowry's *Number the Stars* is a Newbery Award winning novel that tells how a Danish family helps their Jewish neighbors escape the Nazis.

For older students you can read aloud from Milton Meltzer's *Rescue: The Story of How Gentiles Saved Jews in the Holocaust.*

Adapted and reprinted by permission from Cooperative Learning, Cooperative Lives by Nancy Schneidewind and Ellen Davidson. Wm. C. Brown Company, Dubuque, IA 1987, pp. 388-389, pp. 453-457.

Handout 5-12
RESCUE IN DENMARK: A CHORAL READING

A. BACKGROUND

------------------------- ✂ --------------

1. Introduction
Denmark had been occupied by the Nazis in 1940. It was not until October 1943, however, that the Nazis decided to round up Denmark's eight thousand Jews for shipment to death camps. Many people throughout the country acted together as an underground movement to warn Danish Jews, hide them, and then help them escape to Sweden.

------------------------- ✂ --------------

2. This type of action was not typical for most of the countries the Nazis occupied. In many other countries local populations didn't protest the murdering of the Jews. In some cases, they even collaborated with Nazis in the genocide.

In Denmark, people risked their lives to save their Jewish neighbors. Some Danish people died to save Jewish people. Through a choral reading, we will discover how and why they did this. The time is the fall of 1943.

------------------------- ✂ --------------

3. October 29

I am George Duckwitz, a German. I had been living and working in Denmark for fifteen years. After the German invasion of Denmark, I had been given a post in the German Embassy in Copenhagen as head of shipping. I learned that several German transport ships would arrive in Copenhagen on September 29. They would transport Jews, to be arrested in a raid October 1, to German concentration camps. I risked my life to warn Jews of the coming raid.

------------------------- ✂ --------------

4. I am Inge Barfeldt. I work as a secretary. I got word that the Germans planned to round up the Jews. I couldn't warn people on the phone because the phones might be tapped by the Germans. It was almost the curfew time on the night of September 29. If I was caught outside after the curfew, I could be arrested. Nevertheless, I went out with the message to the house of Rabbi Melchior, rabbi of the Copenhagen Synagogue. I knew he would warn his congregations the next day.

B. WARNING

--------------------------------✂--------------------

5. Introduction
October 30

The word of the planned German raid spread quickly and secretly. Throughout the day Christian policemen, postmen, taxi drivers, shopkeepers, doctors, teachers, and students took time off from their work to give warning to their Jewish friends and acquaintances. Being caught hiding a Jew could mean arrest and imprisonment.

--------------------------------✂--------------------

6. I am Jorgen Knudsen, a young ambulance driver. When some student friends rushed up to me with the news, I had to do something. I ripped the telephone directory from the phone booth nearby. I opened the directory and circled Jewish names. I didn't report for ambulance duty that day. Instead, I drove through Copenhagen calling on total strangers to give them the warning. When people were frantic because they had no one to turn to, I piled them in my ambulance and drove them to a hiding place.

--------------------------------✂--------------------

7. I am Dr. Ege, a professor. When a friend told me the news, I took off my laboratory smock and put away my coat. I went to warn all my Jewish friends. Whenever anyone didn't have a place to go into hiding, I offered my big apartment above the laboratory at the school where I worked.

--------------------------------✂--------------------

8. I am Mrs. Ege. When my husband brought me the news, I went out and began contacting all my Jewish friends. When asked why I did it, I explained that it was exactly the same as seeing your neighbor's house on fire. Naturally I wanted to try to do something about it. We hid many Jews disguised as doctors, nurses, and patients at the hospital. We helped Jews because, for once in your life, you felt you were doing something worthwhile. It was a terrible time. Nevertheless our activities gave us a special feeling of oneness. We were together.

---------------✂---------------

9. My name is Mr. Carstensen. I am a conductor on a train. On September 29 a man who rides my train to work came home early. I didn't know his name, but I knew he looked sick. I asked him what was the matter. He said he just learned that the Germans were going to round up the Jews and he had no place to hide with his wife and small children. I said bring them all to my house.

---------------✂---------------

C. HIDING

---------------✂---------------

10. Introduction

In the early weeks of October, many Danes helped Jews hide. Since the Germans controlled the police, radio, and newspapers, Danes didn't know what other Danes across the country were doing. It was only through word of mouth that people could communicate.

---------------✂---------------

11. I am Pastor Ivan Lage. I read a proclamation of the Danish Lutheran bishops in support of the Jews. Part of it said, "Notwithstanding our separate religious beliefs, we fight to preserve for our Jewish brothers and sisters the same freedom we ourselves value more than life." Even though politics aren't supposed to be discussed in church and I could be punished, I added that I would rather die with the Jews than live with the Nazis. I wanted to give my congregation courage to help the Jews.

---------------✂---------------

12. My name is Christian Kisling. At first I didn't believe that the Germans would arrest the Jews. But on the night of September 30 I was wakened by screeching trucks outside our apartment. The Germans broke into the apartment of our Jewish neighbors. Luckily they weren't home. I knew we had to do something. There was a large attic above the garage of the company that I worked for. By the next night we had helped forty Jews hide there.

---------------------------------✂---------------------

13. My name is Gethe Kisling, Christian Kisling's wife. Feeding the refugees in the attic was a problem because I didn't want to arouse suspicions by suddenly buying huge quantities of food at stores where I shopped. So I traveled from store to store making normal-size purchases. I would make sandwiches and coffee and sneak them to the refugees at night. My husband and I sat up most of the night trying to help them keep their spirits up. These were terrible days. It wasn't easy to be cozy in one's own warm bed at night knowing our countrymen were frightened or uncertain about what was going to happen to them, not knowing where to escape, where to turn.

---------------------------------✂---------------------

14. I am Dr. Karl Koster, a doctor at the Bispebjerb Hospital in Copenhagen. I arranged for over 2,000 Jews to pass through our hospital on the way to Sweden. Toward the end of October the Germans started to raid the operating room in the hospital. When a doctor was found performing surgery on a Jewish patient, the Germans would machine gun to death the patient, doctor, and anyone else in the operating room. I had to escape to Sweden and I couldn't return to Denmark until the end of the war. Because the entire medical profession stood together as a single unit in opposition to anti-Semitism, our efforts on behalf of the Jews were much easier. We knew the Germans couldn't arrest all of us.

---------------------------------✂---------------------

15. My name is Signe Jansen. I am head nurse at Bispebjerb Hospital. I convinced our nursing staff to share their nurses' quarters with Jewish refugees. We shared our 130 apartments and donated money to help the refugees. Despite risks, raids, and murders, the nurses continued to help rescue the Danish Jews.

---------------------------------✂---------------------

D. ESCAPE

---------------------------------✂---------------------

16. Introduction

Many Danes risked their lives helping Jews to get out of Denmark. Many were part of an underground network that hid Jews and transported them to safety. Many people were strangers helping strangers, united in a common effort.

17. My name is Peder Hansen and I'm a fisherman. I was approached by a stranger during the first week in October and asked if I could take his two sons to safety in Sweden. I said I would. I also took the fifty other Jews hiding with him. Over the next month, I took many Jews to Sweden.

---

18. I am Ina Haxen. I was a housewife before October 1943. Then I joined underground activities to help Jews escape to Sweden. I acted as a courier. I contacted Jews in hiding and accompanied them to a central point where they would be taken to the boats.

---

19. I am Erling Kaiser. Before October 1943 I was a bookbinder. After that I became a sailor. I never had sailed a boat before in my life. Four friends and I got together and bought a speedboat. I made many secret trips carrying Jews across to freedom in Sweden. I was captured by the Gestapo and tortured, but I gave no information about our secret operation. I was put in a German concentration camp and made a slave laborer. I was lucky to live to the end of the war. Many of the other Danes imprisoned with me died.

---

20. My name is Ellen Nielson. I sell fish on the docks in Copenhagen. Two brothers who sold flowers next to me on the docks asked if i could help them find a boat to Sweden. I hid them in my house. Since I knew fishermen, I arranged for boats to transport them. My sons guided them to the boats at night. I did this for many other refugees. I was caught by the Gestapo and sent to a German concentration camp. The day I was in the line to go into the gas chamber to be killed, word came that Danish prisoners were to be shipped to Sweden. I was saved.

13 THE UNDERGROUND RAILROAD: A Choral Reading

GRADE LEVELS: 3-6

OBJECTIVES: To learn about the underground railroad; to explore the perspectives of different people involved in slavery and antislavery work

SUBJECT AREAS: Social studies, language arts, reading

MATERIALS: Handout 5-13: "Write a Role" cards, one copy of each, cut into appropriate cards; background materials on the underground railroad (see "Going Further" for suggested readings.)

INSTRUCTIONS

1. If your students have some background on the underground railroad, begin by discussing it with them and determining what they know. If they have very little or no background, read or have them read appropriate background materials. (See "Going Further" for suggested readings.) The more background students have, the more independent they will be when you proceed with the rest of the activity. Discuss different types of people involved in the underground railroad and what their thoughts and feelings might have been.

2. Explain that they will be creating and performing a dramatic reading about the underground railroad. First they will need to write it. Assign students to roles and distribute to each student the appropriate "Write a Role" card. Explain that these cards give them the name of their character and a very general description of their role. The students will need to develop a short paragraph that describes what their characters would say. There are questions on the "Write a Role" cards to help them develop their characters. Students who do not have roles can either make their own or be part of the chorus. (See "Chorus" card.)

3. Give students time to develop and refine their characters. Students who play the chorus will need particular help in developing their commentary. Once everyone has developed a role, run through the reading once or twice to determine which areas and characters still need work. Have students revise their roles, then rehearse the reading for an assembly or public event.

DISCUSSION QUESTIONS

- How did it feel to try to get into the head of your character?
- What was easy about it? What was difficult?
- What did you learn about the underground railroad that you didn't know before?
- In what ways were the people in the underground railroad brave?

GOING FURTHER

For background on the underground railroad see encyclopedia articles and the following resources:

National Geographic 166:1 (July 1989).

Charles Blockson, *The Underground Railroad: First Person Narratives of Escapes to Freedom in the North* (Prentice-Hall, 1987). A unique and fascinating resource. Portions of these narratives can be read aloud to the class to help them develop their roles.

WRITE A ROLE

------------------------------ ✂ ------------------------

Calvin Cathcart

You own a large plantation and many slaves. You are known as a cruel slave owner. Where is your plantation? What do you grow? What work do the slaves do? How are slaves treated? Why do they say you are cruel?

------------------------------ ✂ ------------------------

Solomon Richter

You own a small farm and a few slaves. You try to treat your slaves very kindly. Where is your farm? Who lives there with you? What work do your slaves do? Why would they run away?

------------------------------ ✂ ------------------------

Camy Cathcart

You are a woman slave who has escaped from Calvin Cathcart's plantation. What work did you do there? How were you treated? Why happened that made you decide to run away? How do you feel about your journey?

------------------------------ ✂ ------------------------

Rider Cathcart

You are Camy Cathcart's seven-year-old son. You are also a slave who has escaped. What did you do on the plantation? How did your mother tell you that the two of you were running away? How do you feel about your journey? What are some of the things you have seen on your journey?

------------------------------ ✂ ------------------------

Micah Richter

You are a man slave who has escaped from Solomon Richter's farm. What work did you do there? Why would you want to escape from an owner who treated you well? What feelings do you have about leaving? Are you leaving anyone behind?

---✂---

Judith Rowntree

You are an old Quaker woman in Philadelphia. Your house is a stop on the underground railroad. Why did you decide to join the underground railroad? How did you learn about it? How do passengers come to you? What do you do when they arrive? How do you send them on their way?

---✂---

Sebastian Whitmore

You are a wealthy New York City businessman. Your house is a stop on the underground railroad. No one would suspect you of being part of the railroad. Why did you decide to join? Do your family and servants know? What was it like when the first passenger stopped at your house?

---✂---

Rachel Mann

You are a farm housewife in Ohio. You and your husband Joshua have a farm that is a stop on the underground railroad. It was your idea to become part of the underground railroad. How did you first hear about it? What made you decide to get involved? How did you convince your husband to get involved? What were some of the dangers you had to consider?

---✂---

Joshua Mann

You are an Ohio farmer. Your farm is a stop on the underground railroad. It was your wife Rachel's idea to join the railroad. How did you and she decide to join? How do passengers come to you? What do you do when they arrive? How do you send them on their way? Where do they go next?

---✂---

Andrew McKillip

You live next door to Joshua Mann. You don't approve of what he's doing, but you would never turn him in to the law. How did you find out he was part of the underground railroad.? Why do you think he should not do what he is doing? Why would you never turn him in to the law?

Kevin Sharpe

You are a bounty hunter. You capture escaped slaves and turn them in for the reward money. How did you get started in your work? How much money do you make? How do you feel about slavery?

Rudy Scott

You were born into slavery, but you saved enough money to buy your freedom. You are a freedman and you make your living as a blacksmith. You are not part of the underground railroad. Why not? Where do you live? How do you help the antislavery cause?

Cecilia Burgess

You are an antislavery activist in Boston. Every day you work to end slavery. You come from a wealthy family and you still live with them. Your home is not part of the underground railroad. How does your family feel about your antislavery work? Do they ever try to stop you? What kinds of things do you do to fight slavery?

Susan Mitford

You are a housewife on a farm in Virginia. You have just become part of the underground railroad. You have not received a passenger yet, but you hear there will be one tomorrow or the next day. How do you feel about this? What does your husband say? What made you decide to become a part of the railroad? Where will you hide railroad passengers?

Ashton Monroe

You are a wagon driver in Georgia. You are one of the first steps in the underground railroad. How long have you been doing this? How many slaves have you helped to freedom? Why do you do this? How do you hide them?

------------------✂-----------------

Narrator 1

You will need to introduce the choral reading. You will explain to the listeners:

• What the underground railroad was (be sure to tell them that it wasn't a railroad and it wasn't underground)
• How it started
• What kinds of people were involved in it

You might show on a map of the United States where the underground railroad went.

------------------✂-----------------

Narrator 2

You will follow the first narrator, so you need to work together to make sure you don't say the same things. You will explain to the listeners:

• How the underground railroad operated
• How people became involved
• How slaves knew where to go
• The dangers faced by people along the way

------------------✂-----------------

Narrator 3

You will summarize the choral reading. You will need to tell the listeners:
• How many slaves "rode" the railroad to freedom
• Why you think the people in the underground railroad were brave

Chorus

You will provide drama for the choral reading. You should think of phrases, words, sounds, or bits of songs that would make the listeners think of:

• Slaves running
• Being a slave

• Dangers along the way (such as dogs)
• Reaching freedom

14 HUG THE TREES

GRADE LEVELS: 3-6

OBJECTIVES: To learn about a method of resistance through dramatization of an historical event

SUBJECT AREAS: Drama, social studies

MATERIALS: "Hug the Trees" scripts by Sarah Pirtle for three girls and four boys

INSTRUCTIONS

1. Gather a group of students interested in acting in the play. Assign parts and give each actor a script. Provide rehearsal time and direction. The play may be done as a dramatic reading or performed as a play.

2. Have the actors perform the play for the rest of the class. Then they may want to perform for other classes or a school assembly. The actors can learn how to guide the follow-up discussion themselves. It helps to show audiences where on the map the play takes place.

DISCUSSION QUESTIONS

- Why were the people so concerned about the trees being cut down?
- What do you think the wood cutters were thinking about Chipko?
- How is the Chipko movement similar to the sit-ins in the civil rights movement in the South in the 1960s?

Script
HUG THE TREES
by Sarah Pirtle

The Chipko Movement in India

Fictional characters have been created to dramatize real events that took place in northern India villages near the border of China in the early 1970s.

The actions of an eight-year-old girl (named Asha in the play) are factual.

There are parts for 3 girls and 2 or 4 boys.

Girls	Boys
Prema	Rajnar
Kiran	Vivek
Asha	The two lumbermen

SCENE ONE (Two women, Prema, the leader of the women's circle, and Kiran, are teaching Kiran's daughter named Asha)

Song: **All sing together**
Oh where will we go if the green trees fall?
What will we eat? What will we wear?
Where will we go if the green trees fall?
Where will the poor go then?

Prema: The forest is our mother.

Kiran: She protects us with her green beauty.
Here we have our home.

Asha: The forest is our mother. (The two women nod at her.)

Prema: She helps the sweet smelling herbs to grow on the forest floor. We harvest the herbs and sell them at the market.

Asha: (She repeats with greater understanding) The forest is our mother.

Kiran: (She again nods with approval at her daughter)
She holds back the rains. She prevents the floods.

Song: Oh where will we go if all India is flood?
Where will we go? What will we eat?
Where will we go if all India is flood?
Where will the poor go then?

Kiran: My daughter does not know of the danger to the trees.

Asha: Who would harm the trees that are our mother?

Prema: There are companies that want to cut down the trees for money. There was one called the Simon Company. They wanted to cut down the ash trees and use them to make tennis rackets.

Kiran: Here we use wood from the ash tree to make yokes for our oxen–but we would only take one tree and not so many. And first we would pray and sing and thank the tree for its gift.

Prema: The Simon Company came to cut the ash trees in the village of Gopeshwar but the people were ready. They did Chipko and the trees were saved.

Asha: What is . . .? (Before she can finish, Prema continues on.)

Prema: And so the Simon Company tried to take trees from another village. By now they knew that the people were wise and so they tried a trick.

Asha: What was the trick?

Prema: They let the people think that a movie was going to be shown in the next village so that they would leave. As soon as they were gone, the lumbermen snuck in and cut down six beautiful ash trees.

Kiran:	But the people returned and they surrounded the lumbermen. They did Chipko and the lumbermen could not remove the trees they cut and they could not cut anymore.
Asha:	Please, what is Chipko?
Prema:	Chipko is surrounding the trees to protect them.
Kiran:	Chipko is hugging the trees so they cannot be cut.
Asha:	Hugging the trees!
Prema and Kiran:	YES!
Prema:	And now it is time to go to the evening meeting of our village.

SCENE TWO (All five people sit in a half circle. The three have been joined by Rajnar, the leader of the village, and Vivek, the newsbringer.)

Rajnar:	Good evening and welcome. We have two important reports of news tonight. One is very sad. Let us hear about it first.
Vivek:	The Forest Department has marked 2000 of our trees to be cut down and sold.
Asha:	Two thousand! That is so many!
Kiran:	If all of those trees are cut, we will surely have a flood!
Prema:	I remember four years ago when flood washed away all of our fields for growing food and 300 of our winter homes. We cannot stand another flood.
Rajnar:	It will take much careful thought to decide what to do. At our next meeting we will work to think of a plan.
Vivek:	Let me tell you my other news to raise your spirits.
Everyone:	Yes!
Vivek:	For ten years we have been waiting to receive the money we

were promised when our village land was given away to the country of China. Now finally our government says we will be paid. We must travel to the headquarters in Chamoli to receive our money.

Prema: Hurrah. It has been so long.

Vivek: But we are told that we must leave tomorrow. All the men of the village will travel together before the sun is up. Let us go to sleep now so that we can be ready for our long walk.

SCENE THREE (We hear a rooster crow cock-a-doodle-doo)

Vivek: Little one, what are you doing up so early?

Asha: I like to take walks in the early morning. I like to hear all of the animals and people waking up.

Vivek: Wish us good luck. The other men and I are leaving for Chamoli. We will not return for two days.

Asha: Good luck! (Vivek leaves) Good morning birds. Good morning monkeys. And what is *that* loud rustling sound in the bushes? Is it a lion? It couldn't be. Well, I am brave. I'll go and see . . . OH! . . . OH! I must tell the women.

SCENE FOUR

Asha: Please wake up, leader of the women's circle.

Prema: Who is there? Oh, Asha. Come in. What is it?

Asha: It has happened already.

Prema: What has happened already?

Asha: The lumbermen! They are sneaking into our forest while the men are away.

Prema: So that promise of money in Chamoli was only a trick! We will send our fastest runner to tell the men.

Asha:	But the lumbermen are already at our trees!!
Prema:	We women are ready for them. We will use Chipko. Come. Help me awaken the others.

SCENE FIVE (Two lumbermen are deciding what tree to cut first)

Man One:	Let us cut this tall one first.
Man Two:	No, that one is too difficult. Let us start with this other. (The women enter, stand in front of the trees, and hold hands in a half circle.)
Prema:	You will take none of these trees.
Man One:	Get out of our way.
Man Two:	Look! I have a gun!
Prema:	Then go ahead and shoot. It is better that you shoot me then destroy our mother the forest.
Man Two:	(whispering) We can't shoot these people.
Man Two:	I know. I was just trying to scare her. But she means business. They all do.
Man One:	The company never told me how these people feel about their trees.
Man Two:	I'm being paid to cut trees, not hurt people. What should we do?
Man One:	Let's get out of here. They can hire somebody else. (They leave quickly)
SONG:	Come with me now and embrace the trees, Feel the heartbeat next to you. Come with me now and embrace the trees. For our victory now is here.
	HURRAH!

Song
THE CHIPKO SONG

1) Where will we go if the green trees fall?
2) Where will we go if all India is flood?

1) What will we eat? What will we wear?
2) Where will we go? What will we eat?

1) Where will we go if the green trees fall?
2) Where will we go if all India is flood?

Where will the poor go then?

CHORUS:

Come with me now and em-brace the trees feel the

Heart-beat next to you.

Come with me now and em-brace the trees feel the

Last time: For our

Heart-beat next to you.
Vic-tory now is here.

Words by Ghyansham Sailani, adapted by Sarah Pirtle
Music by Sarah Pirtle, © 1984

Chapter Six:
VISIONS OF PEACE

INTRODUCTION

A friend of mine who is involved in international conflict resolution has a vision of peace and peacemaking that I find delightful. Her fantasy is that every time world leaders sit at the negotiating table, each will sit with two babies on his or her lap! "That way," she says, "Every decision made about the future of the world would be made with the next generation literally tugging at the decision makers."

This book is based on the premise that peace is both a dynamic concept and a realistic, attainable goal. All the activities thus far have emphasized these aspects of peace, in part because peace is so often dismissed as "unrealistic" or "idealistic."

It would be a shame to leave the subject of peace without acknowledging one more aspect of it. Peace is also an ideal, and one that has inspired people throughout history. Philosophers and politicians, artists and activists, theologians and teachers, millionaires and Marxists–all have articulated, in one form or another, a vision of a peaceful world. There are several reasons for exposing children to these visions and encouraging them to develop their own.

Some of the world's most inspiring language and art has been created around visions of peace. This is part of children's cultural heritage, and they should know about this work and the context in which it was produced. In addition, seeing or hearing or reading such well-articulated and thoughtful visions of peace inspires children no less than adults. It also shows them that many adults value peace as something worth thinking about and nurturing. Finally, developing their own visions of peace can help empower them to work for a better world in a way they find meaningful.

The activities in this chapter encourage students to reflect upon and respond to a variety of visions of peace. It also encourages them to play with the concept of peace in a variety of media and forms.

Teaching Considerations

Many of these activities connect with the activities in chapter 2, "What is Peace?" The difference is that the "Visions of Peace" activities are a little more fanciful, playful, even magical. These are not the activities for realistically and pragmatically talking about peace. Let your students play with the concept of peace here, and you will gain some interesting insights. Once when I was teaching fourth grade, I did Activity 2: "The Peaceable Kingdom." I had one student, a shy, quiet little girl, who drew her vision of the peaceable kingdom as a large stage, with herself spotlighted in the middle. Around her was all the world, watching and applauding. Her vision of peace told me much about how she wished she could be in the world.

Connecting to Larger Issues

Because many of the activities in this chapter are artistic, provide opportunities for students to share them with others, through bulletin boards, assemblies, etc. This encourages children to see peace as a positive value.

• Students can also share their work with other students around the country or the world. Pen Pal programs and art exchanges are two possibilities. For more information contact:

–International Friendship League. 22 Batterymarch St., Boston, MA 02109.
–International Pen Friends. P.O. Box 14126, B.O. Station, San Juan PR 00915-USA
–People-to-People International. 2440 Pershing Rd., Suite G-30, Kansas City, MO 64108.

I HAVE A DREAM

GRADE LEVELS: (3-4,) 5-6

OBJECTIVES: To familiarize students with Martin Luther King, Jr.'s vision of peace as expressed in his "I Have a Dream" speech; to have students develop personal visions of peace using the "I Have a Dream" concept

SUBJECT AREAS: Social studies, language arts, reading

MATERIALS: Handout 6-1: "I Have a Dream," background material on Martin Luther King, Jr.

INSTRUCTIONS

1. Begin by providing background on Martin Luther King, Jr., and the context in which the "I Have a Dream" speech was delivered. There are a variety of biographies, filmstrips, films, and videos to choose from.

2. Read King's "I Have a Dream" speech (reprinted below) with your students. You might reproduce and distribute copies of the speech and allow students to practice reading assigned parts of it to themselves, asking for help when they encounter difficult words. They can then practice reading their parts aloud with a partner until they feel comfortable. Finally, let them take turns reading their parts before the class, while others follow along. Encourage them to read with appropriate "expression," thinking about the sound and rhythm of the words. Clarify the meaning of phrases the students don't understand. **Note:** the paragraphs of the speech have been numbered to help students locate speech passages.

3. Focus on the message of the speech. Possible areas to explore include the following:

• How is this speech a vision of peace? What was King's idea of a peaceful world?
• What problems did King see in our society? What things did he want to change? What specific injustices does he mention in the speech?
• Do you agree with him? When you think about society as a whole or your life in particular, do you see injustices? Do you see problems? What bothers you about the world, if anything? Is there anything you'd like to change?
• King had many opportunities to accept high-paying, relatively safe jobs. Yet he chose to pass up those opportunities in order to help lead a movement for a better world. That movement demanded that he work virtually all the time, that he live constantly with the

fear that he or his family might be hurt, that he spend time in jail. His work schedule meant that he had very little time to spend with his family. In the end, he gave his life. Why did he choose to live his life this way? What was the source of his commitment to work for justice and freedom? Does his speech give us any clues? What do you think about a person who spends his life that way? How do you think you would have felt if you had been one of his children?

- What about you? How do you want to live your life? What things are most important to you? There are many ways to make the world a better place. Which ones appeal to you?
- How did King work to put his dream into effect? What were his methods? What does he say in the speech about what people in the movement must *not* do? Why do you think he said that? Was he right to advocate only nonviolent methods? How about in your own life? Does his approach have relevance there? What would it mean to live nonviolently?
- What was King's dream, as expressed in the speech? That is, what was his vision of the way the world ought to be? What is *your* dream for yourself? for your family? for your school? for your neighborhood? for your city? for your country? for the world?

4. Have students brainstorm as many individual or shared "dreams" as they can. These can range from the individual and relatively modest ("I have a dream that I could learn to swim the length of the pool") to the local ("I have a dream that the Red Sox would win the pennant") to the global ("I have a dream that there would be no more nuclear weapons on earth"). Don't make judgments on any contributions, even frivolous or self-serving ones. Not all dreams for the future are entirely noble or humanitarian, nor do they need to be. You can gently guide students to more noble dreams as you continue the activity.

5. After all the ideas have been shared, have students write individual lists of their own dreams for the future, starting with the most personal and moving up to the global. They should make their lists as complete as possible, perhaps from ten to twenty items. Encourage them to spend some time thinking about their list, perhaps putting it aside and returning to it over several sessions. Their goal is to define seriously their hopes for themselves, for others, for their world.

6. Have them choose from their lists those dreams which they feel would most contribute to a more peaceful world. Have each student focus and elaborate on these, perhaps by writing a paragraph or an essay or a "Letter to Martin Luther King, Jr." telling about his or her dreams and visions for a better world.

GOING FURTHER

Prepare a program to present before others in the school, ideally as part of the school's celebration of King's birthday. This might consist of selected students doing a dramatic or choral reading of parts of King's "I Have a Dream" speech, followed by readings or recitations of the students' own dream statements.

Bring closure to the "I Have a Dream" activity by having the students choose one of their dreams for a better world and decide on a way they can do something right now to help realize that dream. Joining their efforts with those of a local organization working on that problem is one way; other ways include writing letters to local, state, or national leaders on issues of concern; writing articles for the school newspaper or letters to the editor of the local paper; participating in a walk-a-thon or other fund-raising projects; organizing a student group to work on a school or community problem; preparing an art display on a topic of concern for the school or local library; writing stories or poetry about an issue and sharing them with others. It is important that children have the opportunity to experience themselves as able to take action. We need to help them see that any action, even a very small one, contributes to the combined efforts of others who, like Martin Luther King, have a dream for a more peaceful world.

Handout 6-1
I HAVE A DREAM

1.   Five score years ago, a great American, in whose symbolic shadow we stand, signed the Emancipation Proclamation. This momentous decree came as a great beacon light of hope to millions of Negro slaves who had been seared in the flames of withering injustice. But one hundred years later, we must face the tragic fact that the Negro is sadly crippled by the manacles of segregation and the chains of discrimination. One hundred years later, the Negro lives on a lonely island of poverty in the midst of a vast ocean of material prosperity. One hundred years later, the Negro is still languishing in the corners of American society and finds himself an exile in his own land. So we have come here today to dramatize an appalling condition.

2.   In a sense we have come to our nation's Capitol to cash a check. When the architects of our republic wrote the magnificent words of the Constitution and the Declaration of Independence, they were signing a promissory note to which every American was to fall heir. This note was a promise that all men would be guaranteed the unalienable rights of life, liberty, and the pursuit of happiness.

3.   It is obvious today that America has defaulted on this promissory note insofar as her citizens of color are concerned. Instead of honoring this sacred obligation, America has given the Negro people a bad check; a check which has come back marked "insufficient funds." But we refuse to believe that the bank of justice is bankrupt . . . So we have come to cash this check–a check that will give us upon demand the riches of freedom and the security of justice. We have also come to this hallowed spot to remind America of the fierce urgency of *now.* There is no time to engage in the luxury of cooling off or to take the tranquilizing drug of gradualism. *Now* is the time to make real the promises of Democracy. *Now* is the time to rise from the dark and desolate valley of segregation to the sunlit path of racial justice. *Now* is the time to open the doors of opportunity to all of God's children. *Now* is the time to lift our nation from the quicksand of racial injustice to the solid rock of brotherhood. . . .

4.   But there is something that I must say to my people who stand on the warm threshold which leads into the palace of justice. In the process of gaining our rightful place we must not be guilty of wrongful deeds. Let us not seek to satisfy our thirst for freedom by drinking from the cup of bitterness and hatred. We must forever conduct our struggle on the high plane of dignity and discipline. We must not allow our creative protest to degenerate into physical violence. Again and again we must rise to the majestic heights of meeting physical force with soul force. The marvelous new militancy which has engulfed the Negro community must not lead us to a distrust of all white people, for many of our white brothers, as evidenced by their presence here today, have come to realize that their destiny is tied up with our destiny. . . .

5.   There are those who are asking the devotees of civil rights, "when will you be satisfied?" We can never be satisfied as long as the Negro is the victim of the unspeakable horrors of police brutality. We can never be satisfied as long as our bodies, heavy with the fatigue of travel, cannot gain lodging in the motels of the highways and the hotels of the cities. We cannot be satisfied as long as the Negro's basic mobility is from a smaller ghetto to a larger one. We can never be satisfied as long as a Negro in Mississippi cannot vote and a Negro in New York believes he has nothing to vote for.

6.   I say to you today, my friends, that in spite of the difficulties and frustrations of the moment I still have a dream. It is a dream deeply rooted in the American dream. I have a dream that one day this nation will rise up and live out the true meaning of its creed: "We hold these truths to be self-evident–that all men are created equal." I have a dream that one day on the red hills of Georgia the sons of former slaves and the sons of former slave owners will be able to sit down together at the table of brotherhood. I have a dream that one day even the state of Mississippi, a desert state sweltering with the heat of injustice and oppression, will be transformed into an oasis of freedom and justice. I have a dream that my four little children will one day live in a nation where they will not be judged by the color of their skin but by the content of their character.

7.   I have a dream today.

8.   I have a dream that one day the state of Alabama, whose governor's lips are presently dripping with the words of interposition and nullification, will be transformed into a situation where little black boys and black girls will be able to join hands with little white boys and white girls and walk together as sisters and brothers.

9.   I have a *dream* today.

10. I have a dream that one day every valley shall be exalted, every hill and mountain shall be made low, the rough places will be made plains, and the crooked places will be made straight, and the glory of the Lord shall be revealed, and all flesh shall see it together.

11. This is our hope. This is the faith I shall return to the South with. With this faith we will be able to hew out of the mountain of despair a stone of hope. With this faith we will be able to transform the jangling discords of our nation into a beautiful symphony of brotherhood. With this faith we will be able to work together, pray together, struggle together, go to jail together, stand up for freedom together, knowing that we will be free one day.

12. This will be the day when all of God's children will be able to sing with new meaning "My country 'tis of thee, sweet land of liberty, of thee I sing. Land where my fathers died, land of the pilgrim's pride, from every mountainside let freedom ring." And if America is to be a great nation this must become true. So let freedom ring from the prodigious hilltops of New Hampshire. Let freedom ring from the mighty mountains of New York. Let freedom ring from the heightening Alleghenies of Pennsylvania . . . . But not only that; let freedom ring from Stone Mountain of Georgia. Let freedom ring from Lookout Mountain of Tennessee. Let freedom ring from every hill and molehill of Mississippi. From every mountaintop, let freedom ring.

13. When we let freedom ring, when we let it ring from every village and every hamlet, from every state and every city, we will be able to speed up that day when all of God's children, black men and white men, Jews and Gentiles, Protestants and Catholics, will be able to join hands and sing in the words of the old Negro spiritual, "Free at last! Free at last! Thank God almighty, we are free at last!"

2 THE PEACEABLE KINGDOM

GRADE LEVELS: K-6

OBJECTIVES: To acquaint students with *The Peaceable Kingdom* by Edward Hicks; to have students develop personal visions of peace using the concept of a peaceable kingdom

SUBJECT AREAS: Art, language arts, social studies

MATERIALS: Prints of Edward Hicks's *The Peaceable Kingdom* (Because Hicks painted this subject so many times–over seventy–prints of the various versions are easily available and frequently are quiet inexpensive. Try print departments in museums or department stores. The National Gallery of Art in Washington, D. C. has prints as inexpensive as a dollar. In addition, it is widely reprinted in encyclopedias and art history books. Try to get several different versions of the painting so students can see how Hicks's vision changed over time.) An excellent resource is *Let's Get Lost in a Painting; Edward Hicks, The Peaceable Kingdom* by Ernest Goldstein (Garrard Publishing Company, 1982).

INSTRUCTIONS

1. Begin by having students look at the print and describe what they see. You can prompt them by asking: What is going on in the foreground of the painting? What animals and people do you see? What are they doing? What is going on in the background of the painting? What do you think the people are doing? Can you tell who they are? (They are representatives of the Delaware Indian tribe and William Penn and other founders of Pennsylvania signing a peace treaty in 1682.) Encourage students to be as specific as they can be in the details they describe. (For example, notice that a black child and an Indian child are holding the peace treaty in the background.)

2. After discussing what the students see, extend the discussion: What do you think the people in the background are thinking? How are they feeling? What might the children in the foreground be thinking? What makes this painting a vision of peace? (You might want to point out that the painting is inspired by a verse in the Bible, Isaiah 11:6-9.) With older students, you can focus on the symbolic and concrete aspects of the painting. What are the symbols of peace in the painting? Why would Hicks choose them? How is it a concrete representation of peace?

3. Have students draw a picture that represents their own vision of the peaceable kingdom. Emphasize that they should not copy Hicks's painting, but should come up with a picture that shows the kind of peaceful world they would like to see. Encourage them to include both symbols and concrete examples of peace in their pictures. Older students can also write descriptions of what their personal idea of a peaceable kingdom is like. The pictures and descriptions can be displayed on a bulletin board surrounding the print of the Hicks painting.

4. Have students write about "My Visit to the Peaceable Kingdom." Have them imagine that they were part of the painting for a period of time. Have them write descriptions of who they might meet, what their lives might be like in the peaceable kingdom, how they would spend their time, how they would resolve conflicts, etc.

5. Have students compare the vision of peace described in King's "I Have a Dream" speech with the vision in the Hicks painting. How are they the same? What themes are common to both visions? How are they different? What are some things that a picture can represent more dramatically than words? What are some things you can say in words that you can't say in pictures?

3 PEACE MOBILE

GRADE LEVELS: K-3, (4-6)

OBJECTIVES: To share visions of peace by creating a mobile

SUBJECT AREAS: Art, language arts

MATERIALS: One wire coat hanger for each child, string, 4 x 4 squares of oaktag

INSTRUCTIONS

1. Give each child three squares of oaktag. On the first, ask them to draw a vision of what a peaceful school would be like; on the second, a peaceful town; on the third, a peaceful world.

2. Help the children write a label for their visions on the back of the square. Then punch a hole in the top of each square. Thread the square with string and hang it from the hanger.

3. For older students try this variation. Have them cut each piece of oaktag into the shape of a dove. On each dove have them complete one of the following sentences:

• My vision of peace is . . .
• I will know there is peace in the world when . . .
• I help bring peace in my community by . . .
• My three "Peace wishes" are . . .

When they have written on each of the doves, have them assemble them into a mobile.

DISCUSSION QUESTIONS

• How is your picture of the peaceful school like the peaceful town or world? How is it different?
• What do you want people to think about when they see your mobile?

4 A VISIT TO MEDWYN'S VALLEY

GRADE LEVELS: 3-6

OBJECTIVES: To read about a vision of peace that includes environmental concerns

SUBJECT AREAS: Reading, language arts

MATERIALS: *The Book of Three* by Lloyd Alexander (Holt, Rhinehart and Winston, 1964)

INSTRUCTIONS

1. You may want to read the entire book to the class. If you do not, you can introduce the segment as follows. As you read the introduction, write the characters' names on the board.

Taran is the ward of a good wizard named Dalben. Taran works with Coll, the pigkeeper, and together they care for Dalben's pig, who is named Hen Wen. Hen Wen has oracular powers, which means that she can tell the future. Because of this, the evil Horned King wants to kidnap (pignap?) her. Hen Wen escapes one day, with Taran following her on his horse Melyngar. All three are chased by the Horned King. Taran, trying to recapture Hen Wen, meets with a series of adventures and people, including Fflewddur Fflam, a prince who is also a strolling musician, and Gurgi, a half-human, half-animal who has become Taran's sidekick. Eventually, Taran, Melyngar, Gurgi, and Fflewddur Fflam stumble into Medwyn's Valley, a place of peace and rest for animals–and sometimes people.

2. Read pages 138-155 of *The Book of Three*. Discuss as suggested below.

3. Medwyn tells Taran that it is important for people to learn to help themselves and to learn to help others. Have students describe a situation in which it was important for them to do something on their own. How did doing it themselves benefit them? Next describe another situation in which it was important for them to accept the help of others. How did it benefit them to work with other people?

4. Have students pretend they were following a stray cat or dog one day and together ended up in Medwyn's Valley. Write about: How would you know that was where you were? Why would you see around you? What questions would you ask Medwyn? How would he treat the animals in the valley?

5. Have students draw a series of illustrations to go with parts of the text. The incidents or descriptions on pages 138, 141, 144, 148, and 154 are good ones to illustrate. As an alternative, they may want to paint a watercolor picture of Medwyn's Valley.

DISCUSSION QUESTIONS

- In what ways do you think Medwyn's Valley is a vision of peace?
- What do you think Medwyn means when he says "Everything living deserves respect"? Do you agree with him? Tell why or why not.
- On whom do you think the character of Medwyn is based?
- Why is it important for Gurgi to do something purposeful?

5 ASSIGNMENT: World Peace!

GRADE LEVELS: 5-6

OBJECTIVES: To imagine what types of changes need to occur for there to be world peace; to create a photo-essay about how peace came to the world

SUBJECT AREAS: Language arts, social studies, art

MATERIALS: Handout 6-5: "Assignment: World Peace!," drawing paper, crayons or markers

INSTRUCTIONS

1. Discuss what a photojournalist is and the unique type of reporting they do. Perhaps show some examples.

2. Distribute Handout 6-5: "Assignment: World Peace!" Have students read the assignment and ask any questions. My experience is that this assignment is best done in pairs, but the handout is designed to leave that to your discretion. You may want to give students the choice of working alone or with others.

3. When students have finished their "photo-essays," have them present their work to the class. Post the photo-essays on a bulletin board.

DISCUSSION QUESTIONS

- How did you choose events for your essay? What was easy or difficult about it?
- Which of your events is based on something that actually happened?
- Which ones did you have to make up?
- Which of the events you predicted do you think will actually happen?

This activity was suggested by Carol Reid.

Handout 6-5
ASSIGNMENT: WORLD PEACE!

It is the year 2020. You are a photojournalist for *LIFE* magazine. Your editor has just put you in charge of a special edition that will review how the world achieved peace.

Your job is to collect "photos" (drawings) of the events that occurred between now and the year 2020 and eventually led to world peace. You will need at least seven "photos." Because this is a photo-essay, the only words should be titles and captions for the pictures. Compile the illustrations into a special issue of *LIFE*. Don't forget to make a cover.

Before you begin, think about events that could happen that might lead to world peace.

• What organizations would be involved? What world leaders?
• How would people's attitudes need to change?
• What changes might happen in the economy?
• What would happen to weapons and armies? Would they disappear or would they be used differently?
• Would new organizations need to be created?
• How would leaders and nations be persuaded to participate?
• Did any disasters happen that changed people's thinking?
• Were there any momentous treaties signed?
• How did ordinary people get involved?
• Did new technology play a role?

This assignment has two parts. First, make a time-line of ideas or events that occurred. Show it to me. Once we've talked, you may go ahead and create your photo-essay.

6 TWO FLAGS

GRADE LEVELS: K-4, (5-6)

OBJECTIVES: To explore conflict and peacemaking symbolically

SUBJECT AREAS: Drama, social studies

MATERIALS: Two flags, one white and one red (If you can, have one flag for each student. Then this can be a whole-class activity.)

INSTRUCTIONS

1. Have two student volunteers stand at the front of the class. Give one student the white flag, the other the red flag. (If you are doing this as a whole-class activity, have the students pair off. Then each pair should take a red flag and a white flag.)

2. Give the students the following instructions:

- March your flags to show they are very powerful.
- Have the two flags march toward each other and clash together.
- Have them point and jiggle angrily at each other.
- Have the flags compete with each other to see who can go the highest. When the red flag goes up a step, the white flag tries to get higher, until they go as high as they can.
- Now the flags are tired of competing. Have them collapse.
- Have the flags very slowly decide to become friends.
- Blow on the flags together so that they are equal.

3. Older students (5-6) often enjoy doing this activity with younger students. Give them a chance to try it themselves, then rehearse how they would guide younger students through the procedure and the discussion.

DISCUSSION QUESTIONS

- How did you and your partner use the flags to represent peace and friendship?
- Have you ever acted like one of the flags? What happened?
- What are some ways that countries act like the flags? What countries can you think of that have acted like the flags? What are some ways that people who are enemies can become friends?

Adapted from Helping Kids Care *by Camy Condon and James McGinnis. The Institute for Peace and Justice, St. Louis, MO, 1988, pp. 27-29.*

7 SONGS AND SOURCES

GRADE LEVELS: K-6

OBJECTIVES: To explore visions of peace expressed in song

SUBJECT AREAS: Music

MATERIALS: Song books (see Appendix C)

INSTRUCTIONS

1. Music has been through the ages a popular medium for expressing visions of a peaceful world. Some songs that are popular with children are:
"Last Night I Had the Strangest Dream" by Ed McCurdy
"It Could Be a Wonderful World" by Hy Zaret and Lou Singer
"Study War No More," traditional
"We're All Livin' On the Same Ship" by Betsy Rose
"If I Had a Hammer" by Pete Seeger

2. Older students can have a great deal of fun composing their own rap songs with peace or conflict-resolution themes. This is a good project to undertake in groups. Once the groups have written the song, they can perform it for the class.

GOING FURTHER

Other sources for songs are *Winds of the People* (New Society Publishers) and World Around Songs, Route 5, Burneville, NC 28714, an organization that collects and publishes songs and cooperative games from around the world.

8 WORKING IT OUT IN CARTOONS

GRADE LEVELS: 3-6

OBJECTIVES: To develop imaginary solutions to conflicts through the medium of cartoons; to depict problem-solving and conflict resolution through sequenced drawings

SUBJECT AREAS: Art, language arts

MATERIALS: Handout 6-8: "Tale of Two Donkeys," drawing paper and crayons or markers

INSTRUCTIONS

1. Distribute Handout 6-8: "Tale of Two Donkeys." Discuss with students what they think the cartoon means. Discuss how they might draw a cartoon with people that could have a similar meaning.

2. Once students have some ideas for cartoons they might draw, have them create their own cartoons. These need not be in the style of the "Tale of Two Donkeys." They can be comic strip stories of people or animals solving conflicts. This can be done as an individual activity, or students can work in pairs.

3. Once students have completed their cartoons, post them on a bulletin board. Some students may want to do a series of cartoons or comic strips. When these are completed, they can bind them into a book.

4. Have students look for other professionally drawn cartoons and comics that have peace-related themes. They can add these to the bulletin board display.

DISCUSSION QUESTIONS

- Why are cartoons and comic strips a good way to tell a story about peace?
- Did anyone draw a cartoon based on something that actually happened?
- In what ways is a cartoon like real life? Unlike real life?
- What are some things you can say about peace in a cartoon that you can't say other ways?

GOING FURTHER

Older students may enjoy learning to read editorial cartoons. Have them clip examples from the paper and discuss what they think the cartoon means. Next they may enjoy creating their own editorial cartoons with peace-related themes.

TALE OF TWO DONKEYS

Illustration reprinted by permission of Quaker Peace & Service, London, England.

APPENDIX A

TEACHING CONTROVERSIAL ISSUES TO ELEMENTARY CHILDREN

From international terrorism to toxic waste, from AIDS to the arms race–elementary-aged children are aware of these and many other societal conflicts, but often they are also aware of the sanctions against talking about or even asking questions about such controversial issues. Teachers also have questions and qualms about discussing controversial issues with their students. They have concerns about frightening children, about propagandizing them, and about angering parents or administrators. But then there comes the day when a teacher is having the daily show-and-tell or current events period and a child asks a question about a controversial issue. What should the teacher do?

There are, in fact, many ways elementary teachers can deal honestly and constructively with controversial issues, ways that help prepare children to become the decision makers they are going to be. It might be a simple discussion, or it might be a more structured approach. What follows are some guidelines for discussing controversial issues with elementary children, then two methodologies to help elementary teachers use controversial issues as vital and empowering pieces of their curriculum.

Guidelines for Discussing Controversial Issues

1. Make your classroom a safe place in which to ask questions and discuss ideas.

Before children can ask questions or discuss controversial issues, they need to feel that the classroom is a safe place in which to ask questions or to disagree with classmates without being put down for it. Guidelines for discussion should be established early in the year and reinforced on a daily basis–not just for discussions about controversial issues, but for all discussions. These guidelines should include:

• No put-downs or making fun of other people's contributions
• Let people finish–don't interrupt them
• What gets said in the group stays in the group

2. Listen to the concerns students have.

The most basic job of the teacher is to listen to children's concerns about controversial issues. Don't rush in to correct misinformation or reassure children. First give them a chance to say what's on their minds. As you listen to your students, show that you are interested and attentive. Try to understand what they are saying from their point of view, not just from yours.

What children say may not be what they mean. Sometimes it takes a bit of gentle probing to find out what's going on behind the initial question or statement. You might use such phrases as: "That's interesting, can you tell me more about that?" or "What do you mean when you say 'Killer Rays'?" or "Where did you hear that you can get AIDS by drinking from the water fountain?"

If students seem to be struggling to make something clear, it can be particularly useful and reassuring to have you help them summarize and focus their concerns. "It sounds to me like you've heard some terrible stories about toxic waste and you want to know if they're true."

Good listening also involves paying close attention to what children are *not* saying. Be aware of their nonverbal messages–facial expressions, fidgeting, gestures, tone of voice, or other signals of emotion. It's reassuring to hear adults acknowledge these feelings. "It's scary to talk about nuclear war" or "I get upset about endangered species when I hear about them."

3. Correct misinformation.

One important way to respond to children during a discussion of controversial issues is to gently correct misinformation. The burden of fear and concern children carry about a controversial issue is often due to misunderstanding and misinformation. Keep this information simple and to the point. For example, it's more effective to say simply "There is no one bomb that can blow up the world" than to launch into a detailed summary of nuclear weapons. Follow the lead of children's questions and give no more information than is asked for.

4. Reassure children.

The most reassuring thing we can do for children is to listen to their concerns and take them seriously. Correcting misinformation often alleviates the burden of fear this misinformation creates. And it's always reassuring to children to know that there is someone to whom they can talk–that they are not alone with their concerns and fears.

It is also often appropriate to point out to children that many adults are concerned about these issues and are working to solve whatever problem is under discussion. Children need to know that there are adults who are working to protect them from dangers in the world. If the issue is nuclear war, for example, you can point out that leaders of the United States and Russia have been talking about nuclear weapons and that both countries are even destroying some weapons so they can't be used. If the issue is an environmental one, point out the actions of scientists, lawmakers, and citizen groups. If students ask why there is disagreement among adults about an issue, you can point out that people often disagree about the way something should be accomplished, but that no one wants to see the world hurt or destroyed.

5. Help them find answers to their questions.

The questions of younger children seldom require complicated, technical answers. Older children may well ask questions that stump you. This is the perfect opportunity to ask "How could we find out the answer?" The process of figuring out where to go for information and going through the steps to get it–library research, consulting an "expert," or whatever the appropriate action might be–can be a very powerful and reassuring experience for children. In a small but significant way, this experience can demonstrate for young people that there are orderly ways to go about solving problems and that world problems are not beyond control or understanding.

If a child's questions don't lend themselves to this kind of research process, it is also effective to say something like "I don't know the answer to that question and I'm not sure anyone does. But I know that many people are working hard to solve the problems related to _____."

6. Don't burden children with adult concerns.

In other words, children did not create the problems in the world today, and children should not be made to feel that they are solely responsible for solving these problems. While the temptation to share your own feelings is strong, consider before you do so how that will affect your students. Will it raise new questions and fears rather than help them deal with questions and fears they already have? Another danger is that we might cut off the expression of what's on their minds as we get wrapped up in expressing what's on ours. We might even miss hearing what our children want to tell us.

7. Emphasize that conflicts are opportunities.

Most controversial issues are conflicts, and a discussion about controversial issues is a good time to remind children that conflicts are opportunities. After you have heard and addressed children's fears and questions, they may be interested in the problem-solving aspects of the issue. There is often action children can take that is appropriate both to their ages and to the school setting. Approaching controversial issues from a constructive, problem-solving perspective is one of the best ways to avoid needlessly frightening children, and to prepare them as future citizens.

Both of the models that follow suggest ways to explore many aspects of controversial issues in the elementary classroom using an action-oriented, problem-solving approach.

The Ten-Point Model For Teaching Controversial Issues
Developed by Susan Jones

Summary

In this approach to teaching controversial issues, students begin by pooling what they know and what they think they know about an issue. They also develop a list of questions. This is followed by an information-gathering period during which students search for answers to the questions. Next, using information they have collected, they correct any misinformation previously listed and develop more questions. This process continues until some type of culminating activity emerges from the information.

1. Raise the initial question and have the children brainstorm all their initial responses. Write them down. Don't discuss them, and accept all contributions. Teacher asks only such questions as "What does that mean?" "Can you say any more about that?" "Does anyone else have anything to add to that information?" and (especially for erroneous or extremely one-sided information) "Where did you learn that?" or "Is that a fact or is it someone's opinion?"

2. As soon as undefined vocabulary words, vague concepts, and unanswered questions begin to emerge, begin a separate list of "Things to find out more about." These will serve as guidelines for the ongoing research, and some may even develop into separate topics to pursue later.

3. Information-gathering assignment (homework): Have the children find out everything they can about the initial question. Tell them to "be prepared to share what you can *in your own words.*" It is all right to read articles or watch the TV news, but the best source of information is interviewing parents, other relatives, or friends. Do not copy down anyone else's words–but it is all right to take notes in your own words.

4. Share again responses to the initial question in a brainstorming session. Again, children must share the information they gathered *in their own words*. Write down all responses. Teacher can ask the same questions as in item 1, but offers no information and no "answers." Add to the list of "Things to find out more about" from item 2.

5. Continue the process of gathering information, sharing information, identifying things to find out more about, and going out to gather still more information for as long as the topic seems interesting. Encourage the children to listen to and learn from each other. They can begin to ask each other to explain what a new word means, to elaborate on a concept, to consider a new question, and to state their source of information. The teacher's role is an active one, facilitating, clarifying, and questioning; but the teacher doesn't impose information.

6. If a concept emerges that sparks much interest or confusion, pose it as a new question about which to seek information. Share and question until a satisfactory base of information has been established. More than one line of questioning can go on at the same time.

7. Periodically, give the children an individual written assignment in class to summarize their thoughts about a particular question. The assignment can be worded as "What you know about X," "Things you don't understand about X," "Something X makes you think about," or any other way you can find to help crystallize children's individual thinking about the topic. Sharing these compositions aloud or posting them for all to read helps make all the information public.

8. As individual or group projects emerge, follow up on them. The class may decide to write letters to public figures; one or two children may decide to pursue a challenging research topic to report on to the group; or an outside resource may unexpectedly appear. Be flexible.

9. Let others–parents, your colleagues, the media–know what you are doing. Invite their participation. Encourage dialogue.

10. Let your project end with something either public or permanent–a class presentation to the rest of the school about what they have learned, an article for the school paper or the local newspaper, a class book, or individual books for the school library, or class participation in an event. It is important for children to feel that their learning is relevant and can lead to the ability to make a contribution to the larger world.

Advantages

The "Ten-Point Model" starts where students are and is very respectful of children's knowledge. The process of correcting misinformation is empowering, not punitive. Because students spend time going from whole group to small group and back again, the process is community building and lets all students participate at their own level.

Disadvantages

The "Ten-Point Model" requires that elementary students make use of some fairly sophisticated reference and study skills. There can also be an aimless quality to the procedure if the teacher doesn't present students with some boundaries to their explorations. Even though one purpose of the procedure is to demonstrate the open-ended nature of inquiry, the teacher often needs to structure a clear culminating activity, so that the process doesn't just drift off into an anticlimactic and unsatisfying ending.

Constructive Controversy
Developed by David and Roger Johnson

Summary

In this highly structured, cooperative format for exploring controversial issues, students research and present a point of view on an issue, then switch sides and argue for the opposite point of view. Finally, the group tries to come to a consensus on the issues and writes a group report describing the issue and their combined thinking about it.

Implementing the Constructive Controversy Model

Before the lesson:

1. Choose a discussion topic for which there is no clear right or wrong answer, and for which at least two well-documented positions are available.

2. Prepare instructional materials that will present facts and opinions on all sides of the issue, or will lead students to these facts.

3. Assign students to heterogeneous groups of four. (Heterogeneity maximizes resources and differences of opinion within the cooperating group, which is the goal of this approach.) Assign pairs within each group to opposite positions.

4. Assign each group the common goal of reaching a group consensus and presenting a group report after all differences of opinion have been thoroughly explored.

5. Review or teach the necessary collaborative skills:
• active listening skills, particularly paraphrasing and summarizing another's position
• being able to disagree with ideas while confirming the competence of those holding them
• consensus-achieving skills, such as building on others' ideas, looking for the positive aspects of any idea, and identifying the needs underlying a stated position, etc.

Steps in Constructive Controversy

1. Pairs Study: In groups of four, pairs each study a different side of a controversial issue, gathering facts and preparing arguments. (May consult with like pairs from other teams.)

2. Pairs Present: Each side presents its case; others listen, except for clarifying questions.

3. Pairs Challenge: Each side challenges the other side's arguments, insists on facts, exposes logical fallacies, etc.

4. Pairs Switch: Each side now prepares a new set of arguments and presents the strongest case it can for the opposite side of the argument.

5. Group Discussion: As a group, decide which arguments are most valid from *both* sides, and seek a statement, resolution, synthesis, etc. that incorporates the best thinking of the group as a whole.

6. Group Report: As a group, prepare a report (may be written or oral) for presentation to the class as a whole, to the teacher, or to some other audience. All sign a written summary indicating agreement.

If no agreement can be reached, prepare a minority report as well, and/or a report on areas of agreement and areas of continuing disagreement, including reasons why. All sign this report indicating that it incorporates their views.

After the Lesson:

• Process or reflect on what was learned, in terms of both *content* and *group skills.*
• Give special recognition to examples of creative synthesis of opposing positions.
• Have participants set individual and/or group goals for improving their process next time.
• The group report may be evaluated in terms of how well it incorporates and synthesizes a range of opinion.
• Individual testing may follow, with debating groups being rewarded for the individual achievement of their members (bonus points, etc.).

Advantages

The highly structured nature of "Constructive Controversy" makes it useful for students who respond well to structured situations. The process requires students to make use of collaborative skills, and perspective taking and consensus are built into the procedure.

Disadvantages

Some teachers find that "Constructive Controversy" comes too close to the old debate model. Its major drawback is that issues must be carefully chosen so that there are at least two positions. That in itself is not a problem, but finding material that represents those positions and is appropriate for elementary children can be very difficult. The model requires a great deal of work on the part of the teacher. As with the "Ten-Point Model," students need solid backgrounds in study skills.

Note: Thank you to Nancy and Ted Graves for their help with this summary of "Constructive Controversy."

APPENDIX B

CHILDREN'S BOOKS WITH PEACE-RELATED THEMES

Level and Theme Codes

Grade level codes:
(P) = Primary, grades K-3
(I) = Intermediate, grades 3-6
(I+) = Mature readers

Peace-related theme codes:
(CR) = Conflict Resolution
(PC) = Peace
(Coop) = Cooperation/Community
(Car) = Caring
(Ene) = Enemies/Resisting Evil/War
(Div) = Diversity/Prejudice
(Vis) = Visions of Peace

Books

Anderson, Margaret. *The Mists of Time*. (I+)(Vis/Coop). Knopf, 1984. In the year 2179 a cooperative, pacifist society tries to deal nonviolently with an invasion by violent people.

Armstrong, Louise. *How to Turn War Into Peace*. (P,I)(CR/PC). Harcourt, Brace, 1979. A sprightly nonfiction picture book that introduces the terminology of conflict resolution and diplomacy.

Babbitt, Natalie. *The Search for Delicious*. (I)(CR,PC). Farrar, Straus and Giroux, 1969. The King sends Gaylen out to find a definition for "delicious." Instead he finds conflict and war.

Baker, Betty. *The Pig War.* (P,I)(CR). Harper and Row, 1969. The British soldiers and the American farmers disagree about who owns the island they are on. Based on an actual historical conflict.

Bang, Molly. *The Paper Crane.* (P)(Vis/Car). Morrow, 1985. An innkeeper contributes to peace by folding paper cranes.

Berenstain, Jan and Stan. *The Berenstain Bears and The Trouble With Friends.* (P)(CR). Random House, 1986. Sister Bear finds a new friend who turns out to be more than a little bossy.

Berenstain, Jan and Stan. *The Berenstain Bears Get In a Fight.* (P)(CR). Random House, 1982. Brother and Sister Bear find themselves in a conflict that seems to escalate endlessly, until Mama Bear steps in.

Bishop, Claire Huchet. *Twenty and Ten.* (I, P)(Ene/Car/Coop). Viking, 1952. Twenty French children hide ten Jewish children from Nazi soldiers.

Bronin, Andrew. *Gus and Buster Work Things Out.* (P)(CR/Car). Coward, McCann, 1975. Gus and Buster are brothers who fight continually, until they learn that it is to their advantage to resolve their conflicts.

Byars, Betsy. *The Eighteenth Emergency.* (I)(CR/Ene). Viking, 1973. Benjie has the biggest, toughest kid in school after him–and he has no idea what to do.

Cameron, Polly. *"I Can't" Said the Ant.* (P)(Coop). Coward, McCann, 1961. The ant can't pick up or repair the broken teapot by itself, but if it cooperates with others, the teapot can be fixed.

Clymer, Eleanor. *The Big Pile of Dirt.* (P)(Coop). Holt, 1968. A group of city kids work together to preserve a big pile of dirt they love to play on.

Coerr, Eleanor. *Sadako and the Thousand Paper Cranes.* (I)(PC/Ene/Vis). Dell, 1977. Twelve-year-old Sadako is dying of leukemia as a result of radiation from the atomic bomb blast at Hiroshima. Her struggle inspires her friends, her community, and finally all of Japan.

Collier, James, and Christopher Collier. *My Brother Sam Is Dead.* (I,I+)(Ene/Div/Car). Four Winds Press, 1974. During the American Revolution Tim's brother Sam goes to fight the British against his family's wishes. Soon they are all engulfed by the tragedy of war.

Collier, James, and Christopher Collier. *War Comes to Willy Freeman* (I,I+)(Ene/Div/Car). Dell, 1983. Willy, who is black, female, and free, begins a long search to find and free her mother, who has been taken prisoner by the British during the Revolutionary War.

Cooney, Barbara. *Miss Rumphius*. (P)(Vis/Car/PC). Viking Press, 1982. Alice Rumphius has many adventures before deciding to devote her life to planting flowers along the coast of Maine.

Davis, Andrew. *Conrad's War*. (I)(Ene/PC). Crown, 1980. Conrad loves to play at war. But the play starts to become more and more real, until Conrad can't tell what is real and what is pretend.

De Brunhoff, Laurent. *Babar and the Wully-Wully*. (P)(CR/Ene). Random House, 1975. The cruel Rataxes kidnaps the gentle Wully-Wully. Babar's niece rescues the Wully-Wully and ends an age-old dispute between Babar and Rataxes.

de Paolo, Tomie. *The Hunter and the Animals*. (P)(Vis/PC). Holiday House, 1981. A wordless picture book. The hunter is helped by the very animals he intended to kill. He decides not to hunt anymore.

de Paolo, Tomie. *Oliver Button is a Sissy*. (P)(Div). Harcourt, Brace, 1979. Oliver Button does not act like any of the other boys, but they discover that his differences (and talents) enrich their lives.

Duvoisin, Roger. *Snowy and Woody*. (P)(CR). Knopf, 1979. At the suggestion of a peacemaking bull, two bears become friends and learn to cooperate to protect each other from danger.

Erikson, Russell. *A Toad for Tuesday*. (P/I)(CR/Ene). Lothrop, Lee and Shepard, 1974. The owl intends to eat Morton the Toad on Tuesday, but Morton makes friends with the owl instead.

Erskine, Jim. *The Snowman*. (P). Crown, 1978. A group of children encounter conflict when they try to build a snowman.

Estes, Eleanor. *The Hundred Dresses*. (I,P)(Div/Car). Harcourt, Brace, 1944. Everyone makes fun of Wanda, a poor girl who insists that she has one hundred dresses.

Hansen, Joyce. *Yellow Bird and Me*. (I)(Car/CR). Clarion Books, 1986. Doris's best friend moves away, but she gains a new one unexpectedly when she starts tutoring the thoroughly obnoxious "Yellow Bird" Towers.

Hoban, Russell. *The Little Brute Family*. (P)(CR). MacMillan, 1966. The Brute Family is grouchy and unhappy, until Little Brute finds and brings home a little good feeling.

Horwitz, Johanna. *Aldo Applesauce*. (I)(CR/Car). Random House, 1979. Aldo, the new kid, finds himself stigmatized as weird as a result of several bizarre (and very funny) accidents. Finally he learns how to make friends.

Hunt, Irene. *Across Five Aprils*. (I+)(Ene/Car/PC). Follett, 1965. Growing up in a border state during the Civil War, Jethro Creighton finds himself and his family filled with conflict.

Hutchins, Pat. *Changes, Changes*. (P)(Coop). MacMillan, 1971. Two dolls work together and deal with a series of accidents.

Kellogg, Steven. *The Island of the Skog*. (P)(CR/Ene/Div). Dial, 1973. What is the terrible Skog and how can the mice defend themselves from it?

Kerr, Judith. *When Hitler Stole Pink Rabbit*. (I+)(Ene/Div/Car). Coward, McCann, 1972. A family sticks together during the difficulties they encounter as they escape from Hitler's evergrasping reach.

Langton, Jane. *The Fragile Flag*. (I)(PC/Vis). Harper, 1984. Georgie is a young girl who leads a children's peace march from Concord, MA to Washington, D.C. to meet the president. Along the way they meet many people, some friendly, some not.

Lattimore, Deborah Nourse. *Why There Is No Arguing In Heaven*. (P,I)(Vis). Harper, 1989. The gods bicker about who is greatest until the Creator God challenges them to create a new being. A retelling of a Mayan myth.

Lattimore, Deborah Nourse. *The Flame of Peace*. (P,I)(Vis). Harper, 1987. A retelling of an Aztec tale–a boy named Two Flint searches for Lord Morning Star, who can bring peace to his embattled village.

Lawson, Robert. *Rabbit Hill*. (I,P)(Vis/Car). Viking, 1979. A family of rabbits and their friends worry about what will happen now that a new family of humans has moved onto Rabbit Hill.

Leaf, Munro. *The Story of Ferdinand*. (P)(CR). Viking, 1938. Ferdinand the Bull refuses to fight, despite ridicule and pressure. He stays with his peaceful ways.

Lenski, Lois. *Strawberry Girl*. (I)(CR/Div). Lippincott, 1945. Birdie and her family move into the backwoods of Florida and encounter nothing but conflict from their new neighbors.

Lioni, Leo. *It's Mine*. (P)(CR/Coop). Knopf, 1985. Three frogs quarrel and quibble all day long, but finally learning to cooperate saves their lives.

Lioni, Leo. *Six Crows*. (P)(CR/Car/Ene). Knopf, 1988. The farmer and the crows learn to settle their differences by talking.

Lioni, Leo. *Swimmy*. (P)(Ene/Coop). Random House, 1963. Swimmy and the other little fish organize to protect themselves from the big fish.

Lobel, Anita. *Potatoes, Potatoes*. (P)(Vis/Coop/Ene). Harper, 1967. A mother, distressed by the war in which her two sons fight on opposing sides, brings an end to the war by feeding the hungry troops.

Lowry, Lois. *Number the Stars*. (I)(Ene/Car/Coop). Houghton Mifflin, 1989. In Nazi-occupied Denmark, Anne Marie Johnsen and her family risk their lives to save their neighbors, the Rosens, from deportation.

Mann, Peggy. *The Street of the Flower Boxes*. (I)(Coop/Div). Coward, McCann, 1966. The people in Carlos's neighborhood get together to improve their block.

McKee, David. *Two Admirals*. (P)(Vis/CR). Houghton Mifflin, 1977. Two competitive and egotistical admirals turn a village to shambles as they try to outdo each other. The innkeeper offers a prize to the one who can keep the peace longer.

Meadowcroft, Enid LaMonte. *By Secret Railway*. (I)(Div/Ene/Coop). Crowell, 1948. Twelve-year-old David helps his friend Jim escape along the Underground Railroad.

Meltzer, Milton. *Rescue: The Story of How Gentiles Saved Jews in the Holocaust*. (I+)(Ene/Div/Coop). Harper, 1988. True stories of how ordinary people risked their lives to help Jews escape the Nazi holocaust.

Merrill, Jean. *The Pushcart War*. (I)(CR/Ene). Addison-Wesley, 1964. The trucks are taking over the city streets, leaving no room for the pushcarts. Then the pushcarts fight back.

Neville, Emily Cheney. *Berries Goodman*. (I)(Div/CR). Harper and Row, 1965. Berries and his family move from the city to a small town. He makes new friends, but discovers that grown-ups sometimes have funny rules about who can be friends with whom.

Orgel, Doris. *My War With Mrs. Galloway*. (I)(Ene/CR/Car). Viking Penguin, 1985. Eight-year-old Rebecca declares war on her new babysitter, but soon finds herself actually liking Mrs. Galloway.

Paterson, Katherine. *Bridge to Terabithia*. (I)(Car/Div). Crowell, 1978. Leslie and Jess don't fit in at school, so they create their own world, the kingdom of Terabithia. Leslie's friendship inspires Jess and helps him to cope when real-world tragedy invades Terabithia.

Patti, Clestino. *The Happy Owls*. (P)(PC/Coop/Vis). Atheneum, 1963. All the barnyard animals fight and squabble all day long, except for the owls. They have a long list of things they prefer to do other than fighting.

Pirtle, Sarah. *An Outbreak of Peace*. (I)(PC/CR/Vis). New Society, 1987. The young people in a New England town decide to declare "an outbreak of peace." But the adults don't always appreciate the efforts the young people are making.

Pitts Walter, Mildred. *Ty's One-man Band*. (P)(Coop/Car). Scholastic, 1980. The people in Ty's life are too busy to make music, until the one-legged man shows them how easy it is.

Ringi, Kjell. *The Stranger*. (P)(Vis/Div). Random House, 1968. A giant frightens the villagers. They attack him with stones; his tears float them up to the level of his head, and they are able to communicate and make friends.

Robinson, Nancy K. *Wendy and the Bullies*. (I)(CR/Ene). Scholastic, 1980. Wendy has so many bullies after her that she even has a map of their location. Finally she learns to face her problems with bullies and not run away.

Sacher, Louis. *There's a Boy in the Girls Bathroom*. (I)(CR/Car/Coop). Knopf, 1987. Bradley Chalkers is the worst boy in the fifth grade, always in a fight. But with some encouragement, he begins to change.

Serraillier, Ian. *The Silver Sword*. (I+)(Ene/Div/Car). S. G. Phillips, 1959. A group of young people must overcome their differences as they struggle to escape Nazi-occupied Poland.

Seuss, Dr. *The Butter Battle*. (P,I)(Ene/CR/PC). Random House, 1984. How should buttered bread be eaten? Two nations dispute this and build more and more powerful weapons. What will happen?

Sharp, Margery. *The Rescuers*. (I,P)(Ene/Coop). Harper, 1959. When a poet is made a political prisoner, the mouse Miss Bianca and her friends come to his rescue. Believing that no job is too big for a mouse, they help him escape.

Snyder, Carol. *The Great Condominium Rebellion*. (I)(CR/Ene). Delacorte, 1981. The young people and the old people unite to improve conditions at Lemon Cove Condominium.

Spier, Peter. *People*. (P)(Div/Car/Vis). Doubleday, 1980. The world is wide and filled with different people. Our differences may cause problems, but they also enrich us. A delightful picture book.

Steele, William. *The War Path*. (P,I)(Ene/Div). Harcourt, Brace, 1975. A young warrior learns that war does not promise glory, but pain and death.

Sterling, Dorothy. *Mary Jane*. (I)(Div/Ene). Doubleday, 1959. Mary Jane is among the first black students to integrate an all-white school. At first the challenge seems too much for her, but slowly she makes friends and learns that she has the courage she needs.

Stolz, Mary. *The Bully of Barkham St.* (I)(Ene/Cr/Car). Harper, 1963. The companion book to *A Dog on Barkham St.*, told from the point of view of Martin the bully. Offers insight into why bullies act the way they do.

Sullivan, Mary Ann. *Child of War*. (I+)(Ene/Div/PQ). Holiday House, 1984. A young girl in Northern Ireland learns that she cannot escape "the troubles," but she need not add to them either.

Tate, Eleanora. *The Secret of Gumbo Grove*. (I)(Div/Cr/Car). Franklin Watts, 1987. When Raisin starts to clean up the long-neglected New Africa #1 Missionary Baptist Church Cemetery, she finds more than old gravestones. She finds long-hidden conflicts as well.

Taylor, Mildred. *The Friendship/The Gold Cadillac*. (I)(Div/Car). Bantam, 1989. Two short stories. The first is about a black man in the depression-era South who dares to call a white man by his first name. The second concerns a Northern black family who buy a fancy, gold Cadillac and drive south.

Taylor, Mildred. *Roll of Thunder Hear My Cry*. (I+)(Div/Car). Dial, 1987. Protected by her poor but proud family in the depression-era South, Cassie Logan learns in one turbulent year that it isn't easy to be black in a white-dominated land.

Tobias, Tobi. *The Quitting Deal*. (I,P)(Coop/Car). Viking, 1975. Jenny tries to quit thumbsucking, her mother tries to quit smoking. They continually fail, but keep trying new "cures" and keep supporting each other.

Uchida, Yoshiko. *The Best Bad Thing*. (I)(Car/Coop/CR). 1983. Rinko has to spend the last month of summer vacation with weird Mrs. Hata. After a series of adventures, Rinko learns that people are not always what they seem.

Udry, Janice May. *Let's Be Enemies*. (P)(CR/Ene). Harper and Row, 1961. Two boys who were good friends are now enemies, until they realize that they had more fun when they were friends.

Wondriska, William. *The Tomato Patch*. (P)(Vis/PC/CR). Holt, 1966. Two princes learn the secret of growing tomatoes from a little girl. They take this discovery back to their warring nations, and everyone stops fighting and starts growing tomatoes.

Wildsmith, Brian. *The Owl and the Woodpecker*. (P)(CR). Franklin Watts, 1971. The conflict between the owl and the woodpecker escalates until the other animals step in to stop it.

Williams, Vera. *A Chair for My Mother*. (P)(Coop/Car). Greenwillow, 1982. A grandmother, mother, and daughter cooperate to save money to buy a comfortable chair to relax in after a hard day's work. After a house fire, the neighbors help too.

Zarambanka, Sofia. *Aristophanes' Irene-Peace*. (I)(PC/Vis). Tee Loftin Pubs., 1979. A play based on the Aristophanes story of Irene (Peace), who lives in a cave near a battlefield.

Zemach, Margot. *It Could Always Be Worse*. (P)(CR/Coop). Farrar, Straus, 1976. A Rabbi restores a noisy, quarreling household to peace and harmony.

Zolotow, Charlotte. *The Quarreling Book*. (P)(CR/Car). Harper, 1963. A family has a difficult day, with everyone fighting, until a puppy unites them. (Somewhat dated.)

APPENDIX C

CURRICULA AND OTHER RESOURCES FOR TEACHERS

Abruscato, Joe, and Jack Hassard. *The Earthpeople Activity Book.* Glenview, IL: Scott, Foresman and Co., 1978. An innovative and highly participatory approach to global education. Activities range from art to food to reading to music and games.

Anti-Defamation League of B'Nai Brith. 823 United Nations Plaza, New York, NY 10017. Offers teaching materials on prejudice and discrimination, human rights, and human relations.

Barnes, Ellen, et al. *What's the Difference? Teaching Positive Attitudes Toward People With Disabilities.* Syracuse, NY: Human Policy Press, 1978. Activities designed for teaching about people with disabilities, but are applicable and adaptable to other types of diversity.

Condon, Camy, and James McGinnis. *Helping Kids Care: Harmony-Building Activities for Home, Church and School.* St. Louis, MO: The Institute for Peace and Justice, 1988. An enjoyable curriculum based on puppets and creative dramatics dealing with issues of peacemaking, global awareness, and aging. Some activities need more balance to encourage critical thinking and decision making.

"Decisions, Decisions Series." Cambridge, MA: Tom Snyder Productions. A series of computer simulation games for upper elementary grades in which students make informed decisions about various social issues and see the consequences of those decisions. Designed for ease of use in the classroom. A similar series is available for younger children.

Drew, Naomi. *Learning the Skills of Peacemaking.* Rolling Hills Estates, CA: Jalmar Press, 1987. Activities that encourage children to explore the concepts of peace by becoming peacemakers themselves. A very well-organized and useful guide with many activities.

Educators for Social Responsibility (ESR). 23 Garden St., Cambridge, MA 02138. A national organization of educators that provides training and teaching materials on conflict resolution, peace, the USSR, and teaching about controversial issues.

Elder, Pamela, and Mary Ann Carr. *Worldways: Bringing the World into the Classroom.* Reading, MA: Addison-Wesley, 1987. A carefully thought out and very practical approach to teaching from a global perspective. Lots of activities and resources.

Fiarotta, Phyllis and Noel Fiarotta. *The You and Me Heritage Tree: Ethnic Crafts for Children.* New York: Workman Publishing, 1976. Instructions on making over one hundred crafts from twenty-one ethnic, national, or native groups. Easy to follow for students or teachers.

Fluegleman, Andrew, ed. *More New Games!.* Garden City, NY: Dolphin/Doubleday, 1981. More games in the New Games tradition.

Fluegleman, Andrew, ed. *The New Games Book.* Garden City, NY: Dolphin/Doubleday, 1976. A popular collection of games. Not all are cooperative, but are at the very least reduced competition. Includes an interesting discussion on gaming.

Global Perspectives in Education (GPE). 218 East 18th St., New York, NY 10003. Encourages global perspectives in education through its curricula, training, and publication of a journal.

Grammer, Red. *Teaching Peace.* Peekskill, NY: Smilin' Atcha Music, 1986. A tape of twelve catchy songs about peace and peace-related themes, such as diversity, global perspectives, friendliness, etc.

Graves, Nancy and Ted. *What is Cooperative Learning? Tips for Teachers and Trainers.* Santa Cruz, CA: Cooperative College of California, 1988. The most comprehensive, well-organized, and practical guide to cooperative learning that I know. Activities for use with children and/ or adults. Includes diagnostic and theoretical material.

Hall, Mary Bowen, and Sue Mansfield. *Why Are There Wars? Powerful Ideas for Teaching Writing Skills.* Glenview, IL: Scott, Foresman and Co., 1986. A comprehensive curriculum that includes history, reading, and writing activities for grades 5-8. The activities encourage students to explore war and its causes. A unique and useful resource.

International Association for the Study of Cooperation in Education. 136 Liberty St., Santa Cruz, CA 95060. Provides training and materials in cooperative learning and related concerns (such as peace and conflict resolution). Publishes an excellent magazine.

Kagen, Spencer. *Cooperative Learning: Resources for Teachers.* San Juan Capistrano, CA: Resources for Teachers, 1985. A resource guide to introducing and cultivating cooperative learning in the classroom. Includes many activities along with theoretical overviews.

Kreidler, William J. *Creative Conflict Resolution: Over 200 Activities for Keeping Peace in the Classroom, K-6.* Glenview, IL: Scott, Foresman and Co., 1984. Designed to deal both with classroom conflict and its causes. Includes activities for creating the "Peaceable Classroom" by focusing on the areas of cooperation, caring, communication, appreciating differences, expressing feelings, and conflict resolution. Includes suggestions for dealing with conflicts with parents, administrators, and other teachers.

Luvmour, Josette and Sambhava. *Everyone Wins! Cooperative Games and Activities.* Philadelphia: New Society Publishers, 1990. A handy, well-organized collection of cooperative games, designed for easy use by people who work with children and young people.

National Association for Mediation in Education (NAME). 425 Amity St., Amherst, MA 01002. An organization that promotes the development, implementation, and institutionalization of school-based conflict-resolution programs and curricula.

Opposing Viewpoints Series for Elementary Students. St. Paul, MN: Greenhaven Press. A series of books on current topics that presents pro and con arguments. This is an elementary version of the publisher's highly regarded series for high school students.

Orlick, Terry. *The Second Cooperative Sports and Games Book.* New York: Pantheon Books, 1982. Another excellent collection by Orlick, including games from many cultures.

Orlick, Terry. *The Cooperative Sports and Games Book.* New York: Pantheon Books, 1978. A great collection of cooperative games and activities, organized by age level.

"The Other Side." Cambridge, MA: Tom Snyder Productions, 1985. A computer simulation game for upper elementary grades that requires students to cooperative in teams to build a bridge between two countries.

Pelham, Ruth. *Under One Sky.* Charlemont, MA: Sumitra Productions. A tape of songs about peacemakers and visions of peace.

People-to-People International. 2440 Pershing Road, Suite G-30, Kansas City, MO 64108. Arranges for classrooms in the US to exchange letters and information with counterpart classrooms in other countries.

Pirtle, Sarah. *Discovery Sessions: How Teachers Create Opportunities to Build Cooperation and Conflict-Resolution Skills in Their K-8 Classrooms.* Greenfield, MA: Franklin Mediation Service, 1989. A short but very useful guide to combining cooperative learning and conflict resolution in the classroom.

Pirtle, Sarah. *Two Hands Hold the Earth*. Albany, NY: A Gentle Wind. An ALA award-winning tape of songs and stories about peace and caring for the earth.

Prutzman, Priscilla, et al. *The Friendly Classroom for a Small Planet*. Nyack, NY: Children's Creative Response to Conflict Program. A ground-breaking introduction to conflict resolution and related skills for elementary children. Activities dealing with affirmation, problem-solving, cooperation, and more.

Prutzman, Priscilla, et al. *Friendly Songs for a Small Planet*. Nyack, NY: Children's Creative Response to Conflict Program. A pocket-sized songbook with a wonderful selection of songs about peace.

Rubin, Laurie. *The Food First Curriculum*. San Francisco: Institute for Food and Development Policy, 1984. Designed for upper elementary students, the activities in this guide deal with such issues as where food comes from, why people are hungry, and what can be done about hunger.

Sadalla, Gail, Meg Holmberg, and Jim Halligan. *Conflict Resolution for the Elementary Classroom*. San Francisco: The Community Board Program, 1990. A well-organized collection of activities dealing with conflict resolution and such related skills as communication, emotions, and problem-solving. Includes many unique and useful activities.

Schmidt, Fran. *Creative Conflict Solving for Kids*. Miami Beach, FL: Grace Contrino Abrams Peace Ed. Foundation, 1982. A complete curriculum unit, including worksheets, on conflict and conflict resolution. Designed for upper elementary, but the authors have developed other excellent material for primary grades.

Schniedewind, Nancy, and Ellen Davidson. *Cooperative Learning, Cooperative Lives*. Dubuque, IA: Wm. C. Brown, 1987. A comprehensive guide to implementing cooperative learning in the classroom. Includes many activities designed to develop cooperation skills as well as cooperation and community building as values.

Schniedewind, Nancy, and Ellen Davidson. *Open Minds to Equality*. Englewood Cliffs, NJ: Prentice-Hall, 1983. Activities to help students understand and change discrimination based on race, sex, class, and age.

Schuman. *Art From Many Hands*. New York: Prentice-Hall, 1981. A guide to presenting a multicultural exploration through the arts. Easy-to-follow instructions on how to lead the activities.

"Solving Conflicts." Los Angeles: Churchill Films, 1989. This award-winning 18-minute film shows how a group of elementary children learn to solve the conflicts that arise when they put on a play.

United Nations Association of the United States of America. 300 East 42nd St., New York, NY 10017. Aims to increase public awareness of global issues and the work of the United Nations. Offers many materials of interest to teachers and students.

Williams, Linda Kay, et al. *Caring and Capable Kids: Developing Pro-Social and Peacemaking Skills*. Spring Valley, CA: Magic Circle Publishing, 1989. Activities on caring, self-respect, conflict, empathy, etc. using the Magic Circle approach.

ABOUT THE AUTHOR

An educator with fifteen years' experience, William J. Kreidler is an internationally recognized expert in conflict resolution. He is the author of the highly praised guide for teachers, *Creative Conflict Resolution*, and is the co-author, with Dr. Deborah Prothrow-Stith, of *The Violence Prevention Curriculum for Adolescents*. In addition to his own writing, articles about Bill and his work have appeared in such publications as *Parenting Magazine* and *the Christian Science Monitor*.

As a consultant, Bill has worked with teachers across the US, Canada, and the USSR on conflict resolution, cooperative learning, and other peace-related topics. He is currently working for the Boston chapter of Educators for Social Responsibility as Director of Professional Development. In addition to conducting workshops for teachers, administrators, and community people, Bill also directs the Boston Conflict Resolution Program of Boston Area ESR, a program that aims to reduce violence by teaching Boston teachers and school children new ways to handle conflict.

ABOUT ESR

Educators for Social Responsibility (ESR) is a national professional organization of educators creating new ways to teach for active and responsible participation in an increasingly interdependent world. ESR's pedagogy emphasizes dialogue, critical thinking, cooperative problem solving, understanding multiple perspectives, informed decision making, and nonviolent conflict resolution. In addition to curricula and textbooks, ESR offers training programs that model highly participatory approaches to learning about such topics as conflict resolution and violence prevention, environmental education, drug and alcohol education, the Soviet Union, social responsibility, and others. For information about joining Educators for Social Responsibility, or to receive information about publications and professional development opportunities, contact:

Educators for Social Responsibility
23 Garden St.
Cambridge, MA 02138
(617) 492-1764

ABOUT THE PERSPECTIVES SERIES

Educators for Social Responsibility's best-selling curriculum guide *Perspectives* was published in 1984 as one volume. It is now being revised and expanded to encompass ESR's most recent thinking on teaching and on educational and social change. In its new format, *Perspectives* is now two series of books, *Elementary Perspectives* and *Secondary Perspectives*. *Elementary Perspectives 1: Teaching Concepts of Peace and Conflict* will be followed by *Elementary Perspectives 2: Peacemakers Make a Difference*, which is currently underway. We look forward to hearing your feedback on *Elementary Perspectives 1* as well as any suggestions you might have for future volumes in the *Perspectives Series*. A feedback form follows.

PERSPECTIVES: FEEDBACK FORM

We see this book as a work in progress. Your comments, suggestions and additions will help us revise and improve its depth and quality. We would greatly appreciate your taking the time to share your reactions and any new ideas or materials.

NAME _____

ADDRESS _____

CITY/STATE/ZIP CODE _____

SCHOOL/ADDRESS _____

SUBJECT _____ AGE/GRADE LEVEL _____

1. Which sections of this guide did you use? Which did you find most successful?

2. Which activities worked well for you? Do you have suggestions for improving them?

3. Which activities worked poorly? How could they be improved? Should they be deleted?

4. Overall, how did students react to this material?

5. Did the overview and introductory material help you teach the activities?

6. Did you share this guide with others in your school? What was their reaction?

7. If you have suggestions or activities for future volumes in the *Elementary Perspectives* series, please let us know. (We will list you as a contributor if we use your material.)

Return to: **Educators for Social Responsibility**
            23 Garden St.
            Cambridge, MA 02138